The Divine Liturgy

of the Eastern Orthodox Church

The Divine Liturgy

of the Eastern Orthodox Church

by

N. V. Gogol

Translated by Rosemary Edmonds

DARTON, LONGMAN & TODD
LONDON

DARTON, LONGMAN & TODD LTD
29a Gloucester Road
London, SW7

First published 1960

PRINTED IN GREAT BRITAIN AT THE BOWERING PRESS
PLYMOUTH

FOREWORD

by the VEN. A. P. SHEPHERD, D.D.

THIS exposition by Gogol of the Divine Liturgy of the Eastern Orthodox Church must, of course, be of primary significance and importance to members of that Church, but it also has much to reveal to other Christians and even to the general reader, particularly in the bewildering times through which we are passing.

In face of the rampant anti-Christ movements in the world today the Churches are being drawn closer together in mutual defence and there is a widespread attempt to come to a deeper understanding of one another. In no way is this better achieved than by gaining familiarity with and understanding of each other's forms of worship, and primarily in their expression in the central act of Christian worship—in the west Holy Communion and the Roman Mass, and in the east the Divine Liturgy.

In one way the Divine Liturgy is the most complete manifestation of the mind and soul of its Church. In the west the preaching and teaching of the Word has been largely separated from the celebration of the sacramental act, greater emphasis being laid in Protestantism upon preaching and teaching, and in the Church of Rome upon the sacramental mystery. In the Eastern Church there has been no such

separation, but preaching and teaching are implicit and
explicit in the whole enactment of the Divine Liturgy. In
one sense this may have deprived the Orthodox Church of
the intellectual theology which has been a great feature of
Western Christianity, but in another direction there has
been great gain. Theology in the west has become the special
preserve of the priest and the scholar, but in the east it is
continually presented to the ordinary Christian in a medium
of ritual and symbol which he can understand, in the Divine
Liturgy. It is this fact that has contributed to the survival
of the Orthodox Church in the face of Moslem rule and
anti-God oppression, which forbade the formal proselytising
of teaching.

The contrast between the Eastern and Western Liturgies
goes very deep, far deeper than much that is the subject of
theological dispute. It is a contrast born out of the different
temperaments of Greece and Rome, and the different con-
ditions under which the Liturgies assumed their fully-
developed form. The Divine Liturgy of the east took its
form in the fourth century, when the Roman Empire, which
had accepted Christianity, was beginning to break up into
east and west. In spite of all its enemies and continual con-
flicts, the Eastern Empire remained for a thousand years the
most highly civilised State, with great splendour of Imperial
pomp. Moreover, it was avowedly Christian from the
Emperor downwards, and had a wholly Christian capital in
Constantinople. To the Church this represented the
Christianising of the world, the redemption of Man and
Nature, their restoration to the Divine image which their
frailty and corruption had defaced. All this was seen to have
been achieved by the whole process of the Incarnation,
from the birth of Christ to Ascension and Pentecost, and

this was expressed in the Divine Liturgy in a ritual drama-
tisation of this whole process, in which heaven and earth
were reunited, the worship of the Hierarchies linked with
the worship of man, the redemption of Nature linked with
the redemption of man. It was a divinely-enacted Mystery,
the work of the Holy Spirit acting through the instrument-
ality of the priest, whereby the worshippers, uniting themselves with it, were themselves restored to the Divine image.
While there was constant expression of penitence and
contrition and the claim for forgiveness, the mood of the
Liturgy was reverent joy and thanksgiving for the restoration of man and nature.

The Western Mass came to its full form in a different
atmosphere in the fifth century. The Western Empire had
broken up and was a welter of lawless, warring tribes,
against which the Church stood alone in claiming spiritual
obedience. In the Mass man and nature are conceived as
both fundamentally evil, out of which man is redeemed into
the image of God by the free Grace flowing from the Divine
Sacrifice of the Cross. The whole sacrament concentrated
on the Passion of Christ, by which man's redemption had
been achieved, and this was continually applied by the ever-
repeated miracle in the Mass, of God made flesh and offered
upon the altar. This was achieved, not by the direct working
of the Holy Spirit, as in the Divine Liturgy, but by the
supernatural power of the officiating priest, bestowed
through his ordination, whereby he made God bread and
wine. The mood of the Mass was the submission of the
sinful human will to the Divine Will.

In Western Protestantism the efficacy of the sacrament
to the worshippers was made more subjectively and inwardly
spiritual, and became entirely void of any relation to Nature.

As a result, in the west Nature has become the preserve of an agnostic science, which regards her as purely material and amoral in origin and destiny, and which is making the widest claim to include Man in the same category. Against this the Divine Liturgy, with its repeated presentation of the redemption of Man and Nature from their declension from their spiritual origin to their true spiritual destiny, is deeply relevant to the need of our age.

No one who has been present at the Divine Liturgy could fail to be impressed by the sense of unearthly mystery, but a great deal of the ritual is concealed from the worshipper, despite the continual mediation of the deacon between the celebrant and the congregation. Even to follow the Liturgy in its written form is confusing to the western mind, through the unaccustomed detail of its allegorical symbolism. All the more welcome is this complete exposition through the devout and imaginative mind and soul of Gogol, conveyed to us in this faithful and inspired translation, with its illuminating Introduction.

A.P.S.

TRANSLATOR'S PREFACE

WITH the epic songs telling of the golden age of Kiev under the rule of Prince Vladimir, who converted his country to Christianity in the year 988, Russian literature dates back to the dawn of Slavonic civilisation; but we must wait until the second half of the eighteenth century for the great classics and their peculiar and unique message to the world. With rare exceptions almost all the MSS. of the intervening period are religious in character, the monasteries being the sole repositories of learning. Even in historic records like the *Chronicle* of Nestor every event is seen from the theological standpoint. Later, Peter the Great cared little for purely intellectual activity and what has been termed the renaissance of Russia in his reign did little for literature. The curtain does not rise until the beginning of the nineteenth century—on an era of prose, with Nikolai Vassilyevich Gogol as the leading protagonist.

Gogol came of a family with Cossack connections. He was born near Poltava in 1809. In his last school year he vowed that his life should be marked by good actions for the profit of his country. And at the end he recalled that he had only dedicated himself to literature after realising that he could best serve by writing. (In his most brilliant work he expressed his view of art and the writer's social mission. The writer must 'have the temerity to bring into the open all those things that are ever before man's eyes, yet which his indifferent gaze fails to perceive—the whole dreadful, appalling slimy morass of trivia that have bogged down our life, all that lurks deep within the cold, divided, humdrum characters with which our often bitter and dreary earthly path abounds—and with the firm, relentless pressure of a chisel dare to present them bold and distinct to the general view.')

Gogol's first volume was a collection of short stories in which the supernatural plays a predominant part; but soon he turned his attention to writing for the stage, and *The Inspector*, a satire on Russian bureaucracy, is the second comic masterpiece of the Russian theatre. The play at once became a classic and to this day retains all its vitality and humour. Side by side with his imaginative genius there is a realism based on penetrating observation. Speaking of *The Inspector*, Gogol described himself as writing 'with laughter which is visible to the world, while weeping invisible tears' —words which are inscribed on his monument at Nyezhin, the town where he went to school.

Like all his fellow Russian writers Gogol was obsessed by the metaphysical theme—by the search for inner truth and the salvation of mankind from evil and suffering. They sought the Kingdom of God on earth. With Tolstoy, Gogol believed at first that life could be transfigured through art. His most ambitious work, *Dead Souls*, was designed on the lines of Dante's *Divina Commedia*, to trace man's progress from hell, through purgatory, to salvation. But he could only find a caricature of 'God's likeness' in man, and therein lay his tragedy. Exhausted by internal conflict, he renounced his art as Tolstoy was to do, turned aside from earthly things and died, at the age of forty-two.

Dead Souls is one of the foremost achievements of European literature. Following the pattern of the old picaresque novel, it is an encyclopaedia of the life of the Russia of the time, and bears the same great significance for Russia that Balzac's work has for France and Dickens' for England. In their greetings on the occasion of Gogol's centenary English writers noted that 'Gogol revealed to Europe the quality and the gift which are perhaps the most precious contribution Russia has made to the literature of the world—pity for those who are desolate and afflicted, and wide and embracing love for all who are unhappy and unfortunate.'

Gogol belongs not only to the history of literature but to the history of Russian religious and religio-socialist searching. The religious theme—the theme of the meaning of life and of the salvation of man—has tormented Russian literature, dominating the theme of creative culture. The Russian writer could never stay within the confines of literature. He is possessed by a thirst to go beyond the creation of artistic works to the creation of perfect life. The nineteenth century novelist was a pedagogue with life for his subject, a preacher summoning to repentance and reform.

Gogol was one of the most tragic figures in the history of Russian literature and thought. A Christian who felt his Christianity deeply and painfully, he was overwhelmed with a sense of sin—he was almost a medieval man. Yet there was something even banal about his personal tragedy. . . . He was not alone in suffering so acutely. A genius is a genius only in so far as he continues in thrall to the demon of perfection. In common with the saint the man of genius carries within him the hell of divine discontent. (But here the resemblance ends: whereas the genius despairs, since perfection cannot be achieved by any of the resources at the command of art and must for ever remain unattainable, the saint in silence fulfils the counsel of the Athonite staretz Silouan—'Keep thy mind in hell, and despair not.')

Gogol believed that Russia was called to bring brother-hood to man. He dreamed of a time 'when Europe will come to us not to buy hemp and bacon but to gain wisdom.' With him begins the moral-religious character of Russian litera-ture, its Messianism. This is the great significance of Gogol, over and above his significance as an artist. He is not a realist nor a satirist: he is a visionary, portraying not real people but elementary evil spirit. It has been said of him that he saw the world *sub specie mortis*.

Gogol's treatise on the Liturgy of the Eastern Orthodox Church was the fruit of long study of theological literature and the office of the Liturgy. Probably conceived in Paris in 1845, and carefully corrected and revised shortly before his death, it was not published until five years later. He wanted it to be a small octavo book, a 'popular' edition selling cheaply and not bearing his name. He was convinced that Russia's hope lay in a 'more genuinely religious life, in austerity, self-sacrifice, and obedience to constituted authority.' He preached moral perfection, without which he saw no possibility of achieving Utopia. But 'not to be happy, not to rejoice in spirit is a sin. . . . Our whole life ought to be an unceasing joyous hymn of gratitude to God.' He hoped that his *Divine Liturgy* would instruct and edify, and he died 'persuaded that the Liturgy's deep inner meaning will unfold itself naturally to everyone who listens atten-tively, repeating each word in his heart.' Groaning creation's cry had been heard. 'There appeared among us One like unto us . . . not in proud splendour and majesty, not as the avenger of wickedness, not as a judge come to destroy some and reward others. No. He came with the gentle kiss of a brother . . .' There we have Gogol's *Nunc Dimittis*: he has learned of Christ's mercy and forgiveness—now he knows Christ as the Redeemer—and his soul is filled with joy.

In his spiritual testament Gogol bids his 'friends'—that is, all Russians—not to be dead but living souls. 'There is no other way than through Jesus Christ.' These were his last words, and they reveal the secret of his existence. He saw God as the infinite, the beginning and the end, and the devil as the negation of God, and so of the infinite, the negation of all beginning and all end; the devil is the begun and the unfinished passing for the infinite, the negation of all height and depth—the eternal platitude, the eternal commonplace. The whole force of his work was directed against the devil under this aspect.

It was Gogol's tragedy that whereas his spiritual vision of Christ required him to overcome his art and stand outside its confines he attempted the contrary—he tried to compress Christ into art, to fit his spiritual vision into his work as a writer. He could not renounce his art and live, and therefore his strange death, almost from insanity, came as a logical and inevitable conclusion. Many poets and men of genius have ended their lives by suicide.

Although Gogol can scarcely be said to have resolved a single issue in the realm of art he nevertheless opened the way to future writers; without him such masters as Tolstoy and Dostoyevsky could not have followed. Gogol converted Russian literature from romanticism to realism, permeating the realistic definition which he created with a feeling of deep-stirring energies, hopes, revolts, aspirations. But above all he turned the faces of his contemporaries and heirs to Religion.

NOTES

1. The word 'Liturgy', which in the Greek means a 'public work' or 'ministry', is particularly applied to the chief service of the day, in which the Holy Eucharist is celebrated, recalling the whole sacrificial life of Christ, from Bethlehem to Pentecost. The Eastern Orthodox Church—which is comprised of a number of autocephalous national churches, each using its own language and preserving its own customs and traditions—knows three main liturgical rites. (A fourth, the Liturgy of St James the Apostle, is celebrated only once a year, on his feast, and then only in Jerusalem.) The text Gogol interprets is that of St John Chrysostom (born *c.* 347), which is a later and abbreviated form of St Basil's Liturgy, just as the latter, in turn, was a later and abbreviated form of a still earlier liturgy.

2. The marginal references have been added by the translator, who has used the Authorized Version for all Biblical quotations, although the Slavonic text of the Liturgy in the Russian Orthodox Church quotes from the Septuagint.

3. Although recently in certain churches there has been some revival of congregational singing, the congregation does not now, as a rule, join vocally in the responses. The faithful 'echo the choir' in thought and intention rather than literally.

In the present text those passages of the Liturgy which are spoken aloud by priest or deacon (or sung by the choir) and heard by the congregation are printed in italics.

R.E.

INTRODUCTION

The purpose of this book is to acquaint young people and others with the fullness and profound inward coherence of our Liturgy. From the many commentaries by the Fathers and Doctors of the Church the author has selected only such as are universally intelligible by reason of their simple clarity—those which most conduce to an understanding of the true and inevitable progression of the service. He would impress on the reader the ordered sequence of the whole, persuaded that the deep inner meaning of the Liturgy will unfold itself naturally to everyone who listens attentively, repeating each word in his heart.

The Divine Liturgy is a continual repetition of the great feat of love which was performed for us. From the far corners of the earth all mankind—the heathen worshipping his idols alike with the ignorant of God—in sorrow for their disordered state had invoked the Creator, sensing that order and harmony could be established in the world only by Him who had bidden His universe observe the music of the spheres. Groaning creation called to its Creator. Unceasing lamentation rose to the Author of man's being. Loudest of all was the cry of mankind in the mouths of the elect and of the prophets. They foresaw, they knew, that the Creator concealed behind creation would appear to man—would appear no otherwise than in the form of His creature made after His own image and likeness. As their apprehension of the Divinity clarified, so did men come to expect the Incarnation of God on earth, which the prophets of the chosen people proclaimed more certainly than all others. His most pure Incarnation of a pure Virgin was foretold even by the heathen; but by no one so plainly as by the prophets.

The cries were heard: He by Whom the world was made appeared in the world. There appeared among us One like unto us, as the heathen had foreknown in his darkness—but not as the heathen with his unenlightened understanding had expected: not in proud splendour and majesty, not as the avenger of wickedness, not as a judge come to destroy some and reward others. No. He came with the gentle kiss of a brother. He came as only God could come, as the prophets who had been inspired by God had represented Him, divinely. . . .

i

THE OFFERTORY,
OR OFFICE OF OBLATION

THE priest who is to celebrate the Liturgy must from the evening before hold himself sober and recollected in mind and body. He should be reconciled with all men and take care that he bears no ill will towards anyone. When the time is come he enters the church, and he and the deacon bow themselves before the Royal Gates.[1] They both kiss the ikons of the Saviour and the Mother of God, bow before the ikons of the saints, bow to right and to left to all present, thereby asking forgiveness of all, and enter the sanctuary, repeating to themselves verses from the fifth Psalm: 'I will come into thy house . . . in thy fear will I worship toward thy holy temple.' Approaching the altar, they prostrate themselves three times, their faces turned towards the east, and kiss the Gospel book lying on the altar as though it were the Lord Himself sitting upon the throne. Then they kiss the holy table, before proceeding to robe in the sacred vestments which are to distinguish them not only from other people but even from their usual selves: their appearance must in nothing recall men occupied with the everyday business of life. Repeating within themselves

[1] The Royal Gates—so called because through them the King of Glory comes forth to feed his faithful people with His own Divine Body and Blood—are only opened for ceremonial entrance and exit. At all other times the north and south doors in the ikonostasis (the screen) are used. [Tr.]

'O God, cleanse Thou me a sinner, and have mercy upon me', the priest and the deacon take their vestments in their hands.

The deacon is the first to robe. Having asked the priest's blessing, he puts on the alb, which is always light in colour to signify the bright raiment of an angel and in token of the unsullied purity of heart which should be inseparable from the priestly office. Wherefore as they vest in alb or dalmatic both priest and deacon say: 'My soul shall be joyful in my God; for he hath clothed me with the garments of salvation, he hath covered me with the robe of righteousness, as a bridegroom decketh himself with ornaments, and as a bride adorneth herself with her jewels.' (*Isa. lxi*, 10.) Then, having kissed the stole, a long narrow band, the deacon hangs it over his left shoulder. This stole, or *orarion*, is the particular attribute of the diaconate. With it the deacon conducts the service, calling on the people to pray, the choir to sing, the priest to perform the sacerdotal acts, and himself to be swift and ready as the angels to serve. For the office of the deacon is like that of the angels in heaven, the slender ribbon light as a wing on his shoulder and his rapid movements about the church suggesting, in the words of St John Chrysostom, the flying of an angel. Next the deacon puts on the cuffs, which fasten round the wrist in order to give his hands greater freedom and dexterity in the performance of their appointed service. While putting on the cuffs he reflects on the all-creating might of God operating in every place. As he fastens the right one he repeats: 'Thy right hand, O Lord, is become glorious in power: thy right hand, O Lord, hath dashed in pieces the enemy. And in the greatness of thine excellency thou hast overthrown them that rose up against thee.' (*Exod. xv*, 6, 7.) Putting on the left cuff he reflects on himself as the work of God's hands, and prays to his Creator to guide him with His sovereign guidance from on high, saying thus: 'Thy hands have made me and fashioned me: give me understanding, that I may learn thy commandments.' (*Ps. cxix*, 73.)

The priest vests in the same manner. He first blesses and puts on the alb, accompanying this with the same words as those used by the deacon; but following the alb he puts on not a simple stole over one shoulder but a double one called the *epitrakhelion*, which, going round the neck and over both shoulders, meets and is joined together on the breast, to continue as one piece down to the hem of his garment, the conjunction signifying the union of the two offices of priest and deacon. The putting on of the *epitrakhelion* symbolises the pouring out of grace from on high upon the priest, and so is accompanied by the august words of Scripture: 'Blessed is God who poureth out his grace upon his priests, like the precious ointment upon the head, that ran down upon the beard, even Aaron's beard: that went down to the skirts of his garments.' (*Ps. cxxxiii*, 2.) Then he puts the cuffs upon his hands, repeating the same words as the deacon used, girds himself with the girdle over the alb and *epitrakhelion*, that the fullness of his vestments may not hinder the accomplishment of the sacerdotal acts, and by thus girding himself to express his preparedness; for even as a man girds himself when making ready for a journey or embarking upon some task, so too does the priest gird himself before starting on his heavenly office. Looking upon the girdle as the power of God's might strengthening him, he saith: 'Blessed is God that girdeth me with strength, and maketh my way perfect. He maketh my feet like hinds' feet, and setteth me upon my high places' (*Ps. xviii*, 32, 33), that is, in the house of the

Lord. Then, if he has been ordained into the higher priest-hood, he hangs at his side by one of its four corners the four-square *epigonation*, symbol of the spiritual sword, the all-conquering power of the Word of God, declaring the perpetual combat facing men in this world, the victory over death which Christ gained in the eyes of the whole world, that the immortal spirit of man might fight bravely against his corruption. Therefore the *epigonation* has the appearance of a puissant weapon of war, and is hung upon the girdle, at the loins, the seat of man's strength, and its putting on is accompanied by an invocation to the Lord Himself: 'Gird thy sword upon thy thigh, O most mighty, with thy glory and thy majesty. And in thy majesty ride prosperously be-cause of truth and meekness and righteousness; and thy right hand shall teach thee terrible things.' (*Ps. xlv*, 3, 4). Finally, over his other vestments the priest puts on the chasuble, signifying the all-covering truth of God, and saith: 'Let thy priests, O Lord, be clothed with righteousness; and let thy saints shout for joy.' (*Ps. cxxxii*, 9.) Thus vested with the instruments of God, the priest appears transformed: whatever he be in himself, how little worthy of his calling, the faithful standing in the church behold in him the instrument of God wielded by the Holy Spirit. Both priest and deacon wash their hands, while repeating the psalm, 'I will wash mine hands in innocency: so will I compass thine altar.' (*Ps. xxvi*, 6.) Then, making three lowly rever-ences, each saith: 'O God, cleanse Thou me a sinner, and have mercy upon me', and they stand, cleansed and radiant like their raiment, in nothing resembling other people but more like a shining vision than men.

The deacon indicates the commencement of Divine Ser-vice: 'Master, pronounce a blessing!' and the priest begins with the words: 'Blessed is our God, always, now and for ever and unto ages of ages', and proceeds to the side altar. All this part of the service consists in the preparation of what is required for the celebration, i.e. in the separation from the gifts, or little loaves of bread, of those sections which at first represent and are later to become the Body of Christ.

As the whole Office of Oblation is nothing else than a preparation for the Liturgy, the Church commemorates with it the preliminary period of Christ's life, as being the prelude to His work, suffering and death. All is done within the sanctuary with closed doors and drawn curtain, unseen of the people, even as the whole of the early life of Christ passed unseen of the multitude. During the Offertory the Hours are read to the worshippers. These are collections of psalms and prayers used by the primitive Christians to mark the four cardinal times of the day: the first hour when for Christians the morning began; the third hour, the coming down of the Holy Spirit; the sixth hour when the Saviour of the world was nailed to the Cross; and the ninth hour, when He gave up the ghost. As it is not possible for us today, pressed for time and beset by distractions, to perform these devotions at their appointed hours, they are linked together and read now.

Proceeding to the side altar, or place of offering, which is situated in a recess in the wall and represents the prothesis in primitive churches, the priest takes one of the little loaves of altar bread, called *prosphori*, in order to separate from it the section which will later become the Body of Christ—the middle portion of the upper part, on which is the seal bearing the name of Jesus Christ. This separating of bread from bread symbolises the separating of the flesh of Christ from the flesh of the Virgin—the birth in the flesh of Him Who was incorporeal. Meditating that now He is born Who offered Himself in sacrifice for the whole world, the priest remembers the sacrifice too, and sees in the bread the Lamb brought for sacrifice, in the knife with which he must divide it (which has the form of a spear in commemoration of the spear which pierced the Body of the Saviour upon the Cross) the sacrificial knife. He does not now repeat any words of the Saviour or His contemporaries. Nor are his thoughts directed to the day when the sacrifice was offered —that is still to come, in the latter part of the Liturgy, and to that which is to come he turns his thoughts as into a far future. Wherefore all his acts are accompanied by words taken from the prophet Isaiah who, out of the darkness of the ages, looked forward and saw the wondrous birth, the sacrifice and death, which he proclaimed with searchless clarity. Thrusting the spear into the right side of the seal, the priest says: 'He is brought as a lamb to the slaughter.' (*Isa. liii*, 7.) Then into the left side, saying: 'And as a sheep before her shearers is dumb, so he openeth not his mouth.' At the top of the seal, saying: 'He was condemned for his humility, he was taken . . . from judgment.' At the bottom, saying—while he ponders deeply on the wondrous origin of the condemned Lamb—'And who shall declare his generation?' Then with the spear he lifts out the middle section of the bread which has been cut round, saying: 'For he was cut off out of the land of the living'; (*Isa. liii*, 8.) and, in token of His death upon the Cross, traces the sign of sacrifice on it, uttering the words: 'The Lamb of God, which taketh away the sin of the world, for the life and salvation of the world.' (*John i*, 29.) (Following the lines of the cross which he has traced, the priest will afterwards divide the bread.) And having turned the bread over so that the seal is face downwards and the lower part uppermost, in the likeness of the lamb brought to the sacrifice, he thrusts the spear into the right side, remembering together with the slaying of the victim the piercing of the Redeemer's side with the spear of the soldier who stood near the Cross, and repeats: 'One of the soldiers with a spear pierced his side, and forthwith came there out blood and water. And he that saw it bare record, and his record is true.' (*John xix*, 34, 35.) These words serve also as a sign to the deacon to pour wine and water into the chalice. The deacon who all this time has been a reverent witness of these actions of the priest's, the while repeating to himself: 'Let us pray to the Lord', now pours wine and water into the chalice, asking the blessing of the priest upon the union. Thus are the wine and the bread prepared for that which they are to become during the subsequent great Mystery.

Then, in completion of the rite of the Primitive Church and of the first Christian saints who when they thought of Christ remembered always those who were near to His heart for their fulfilment of His commandments and the holiness of their lives, the priest proceeds to take portions from other *prosphori*, in their memory, and places them upon the same paten near the holy Bread which represents the Lord Himself, for they burned with the desire to be everywhere with their Lord. Taking in his hand a second *prosphora*, he cuts from it a portion commemorating the most holy Mother of God and places it on the right side of the Lamb, repeating the words of the Psalmist: 'Upon thy right hand did stand the queen in clothing wrought with gold and divers colours.' (*Ps. xlv*, 9.) Then he takes a third *prosphora*, to commemorate the saints, and with the same spear separates from it nine portions in three rows of three. The first portion in honour of St John the Baptist, the second of the prophets, the third of the apostles; and thus is formed the first row and rank of saints. Then he separates a fourth particle in remembrance of the holy fathers, a fifth for the martyrs, a sixth for the reverend fathers and matrons who bore God in their hearts; and thus is formed the second row and rank of saints. Then he separates a seventh portion in the name of the workers of miracles and the self-denying, an eighth in the name of the forefathers of God, Joachim and Anna, and of the saint whose feast day it is, a ninth in the name of St John Chrysostom or St Basil the Great, according to which Liturgy is being celebrated; and thus is formed the third row and rank of holy ones. And all the nine portions are placed on the paten, near the Lamb, on the left side of It.

Thus Christ appears among His own: He Who inhabiteth the saints is seen among His holy ones—God among gods, Man among men. And taking in his hand a fourth *prosphora* for all the living, the priest separates from it a particle in the name of the Emperor, another for the Synod,[1] a third particle for all Orthodox Christians far and wide, and lastly, a particle for those he wishes to pray for by name or whom he has been asked to remember. Finally the priest takes a fifth and last *prosphora* and separates from it portions in commemoration of all the dead, asking for forgiveness of their sins, beginning with patriarchs, tsars, the founders of the church in which he is officiating, for the bishop who ordained him, if he be among those who have departed this life, down to the least Christian, separating a particle for each one for whom he has been asked to pray or whom he

---

[1] Now—'our Patriarch N., our Archbishop (or Bishop) N. and every order of clergy'. [*Tr.*]

himself wishes to commemorate. And last of all he asks for forgiveness for his own sins, and likewise separates a portion for himself; and all these portions the priest places on the paten below the Bread Which is the Lamb. Thus around this Bread Which is the Lamb, representing Christ Himself, is gathered His whole Church, both triumphant in heaven and militant on earth. The Son of Man appears among men, for whose sake He became incarnate and was made Man. With the sponge the priest carefully brushes the very crumbs together upon the paten, that nothing of the sacred bread be lost, that all be secure.

Standing back from the offertory table, the priest prostrates himself as though to the Incarnate Christ, and honours, in the form of the bread lying upon the paten, the manifestation on earth of the Heavenly Bread, to Which he does homage by censing with the censer—he has already blessed the censer with the prayer: 'We offer incense unto Thee, O Christ our God, for a sweetsmelling savour of spiritual fragrance, which do Thou accept upon Thy most heavenly altar, and send down upon us in return the grace of Thy most holy Spirit.' [cf. *Eph. v,* 2.]

Then, transporting himself in thought to the time of the Nativity of Christ, and bringing the past forward into the present, the priest looks upon the altar of oblation as though it were the mystic grotto wherein heaven came down to earth: when heaven became a grotto and a grotto became heaven. Having censed the asterisk,[1] or star—two curved shafts of gold with a star above—and setting it over the paten, he sees it like the star which shone above the place

---

[1] In the Byzantine rites, a utensil consisting of two metal strips crossed and bent and placed over the blessed bread during the Liturgy to keep it from contact with the veil that covers it (O.D.C.C.). [*Tr.*]

where the Child lay, saying, as he does so, 'And the star . . . came and stood over where the young child was.' (*Matt. ii*, 9.) In the Bread separated for the sacrifice the priest sees the new-born Babe. The paten is the manger where the Child lay. The veils are the swaddling-clothes in which the Child was wrapped. Censing the first veil, he covers the holy bread and the paten, while he says the psalm: 'The Lord reigneth, he is clothed with majesty . . .' (*Ps. xciii*, 1) and so on—the psalm in praise of the wondrous nobility of God. Censing the second veil, he covers the chalice, saying 'Thy virtue, O Christ, covered the heavens, and the earth was full of thy praise.' [cf. *Hab. iii*, 3.] Then, taking the large veil, called the *aer*, he covers with it both paten and chalice, calling upon God to spread over us the shelter of His wing. Standing back from the oblation, both priest and deacon bow themselves before the Holy Bread as the shepherds and kings bowed before the new-born Child, and the priest censes the altar-cave, in token of the sweet-smelling incense, the myrrh and the gold which the wise men brought.

The deacon, as before, attentively accompanies the priest, now repeating 'Let us pray to the Lord', now inspiring him to the next act. Finally he receives the censer from the priest's hand, and with the words 'For the precious gifts here set forth, let us pray to the Lord' indicates the prayer to be lifted up to the Lord for the gifts made ready for Him; and the priest begins the Prayer of Oblation. Although these gifts are, so far, only prepared for the sacrifice, still, as they can now no longer be put to any other use, the priest prays to himself the prayer which precedes their acceptance: 'O God, our God, Who didst send unto us Jesus Christ, our Lord and God, our Saviour, Redeemer and Benefactor, by Whom we are hallowed and blessed, to be bread from heaven, to be food for the whole world, do Thou bless this oblation here set forth and receive it unto Thy most heavenly altar. Remember of Thy goodness and loving-kindness them by whom and for whom these things are brought; and preserve us that without condemnation we may celebrate Thy divine mysteries.' Whereupon he pronounces the dismissal at the end of the Office of Oblation, while the deacon censes first the offerings and then the holy table round about, in the form of a cross. Meditating on the birth into the world of Him Who was begotten before all worlds, and is always and everywhere present, the deacon repeats within himself: 'While in the tomb according to the flesh, Thou yet, being God, wast with Thy spirit in hell, in paradise with the thief, and with the Father and the Holy Ghost on the throne, O Christ incircumscriptable, Thou Who dost fill all things.' He leaves the sanctuary, censer in hand, to fill the whole church with fragrance, and greet all who are gathered together before the sacred table of love. This censing is performed at the beginning of each service, in the same way as in the domestic life of all the ancient peoples of the East every guest when he arrived was offered ablution and perfume. So the custom is continued in the heavenly feast, the Lord's Supper, which is called the Liturgy—a service most wondrously uniting worship of God and friendly hospitality to all, after the manner of the Saviour Himself, Who waited upon and washed the feet of every man. Censing and bowing to all alike, rich and poor, the deacon, as the servant of God, greets them all as the most welcome guests of the heavenly Host. He censes and bows at the same time before the ikons of the saints, for they too are guests come to the Lord's Supper: for in

Christ all have life inseparable. Having made ready and filled the church with fragrance, the deacon returns to the sanctuary and, after censing it again, lays the censer aside and goes up to the priest. Standing together before the altar, priest and deacon bow themselves three times, and, preparing now to begin the Divine Office of the Liturgy, invoke the Holy Spirit, for all that they do must be done of the spirit. The Holy Spirit is Teacher and Preceptor of prayer. 'For we know not what we should pray for as we ought,' says St Paul, 'but the Spirit itself maketh intercession for us with groanings which cannot be uttered.' (*Rom. viii*, 26.) Entreating the Holy Spirit to descend and rest upon them, and purify them for their service, priest and deacon repeat twice the song with which the angels greeted the Nativity of Jesus Christ: 'Glory to God in the highest, and on earth peace, good will toward men.' (*Luke ii*, 14.) And immediately after, they draw back the curtain from the Royal Gates. This curtain is always drawn back as a sign to the congregation to lift their minds to high and celestial matters. Here the opening of the curtain over the Royal Gates after the angels' hymn signifies that the birth of Christ was not revealed to all, that it was known only to the angels in heaven, to Mary and Joseph, to the wise men who came to worship—and to the prophets who foresaw from afar. Priest and deacon repeat within themselves: 'O Lord, open thou my lips; and my mouth shall shew forth thy praise.' (*Ps. li*, 15.) The priest kisses the book of the Gospels, the deacon kisses the holy table, and by bowing his head to the priest indicates the beginning of the Liturgy. Holding his stole with three fingers, he says: 'It is time for thee, Lord, to work. (*Ps. cxix*, 126.) Father, give me your blessing.' And the priest blesses him with the words 'Blessed is our

God, always, now and for ever and unto ages of ages.'
The deacon, meditating on the office which is before him,
in which he must be like unto an angel flying from the altar
to the people, and from the people to the altar, gathering
all together and making them of one spirit—in which he
must be, as it were, a holy inspiring power—and conscious
of his unworthiness for such service, humbly asks of the
priest: 'Pray for me, holy Father.'—'May the Lord direct
thy steps!' the priest answers him. 'Remember me, holy
Father.'—'May the Lord remember thee in His kingdom,
always, now and for ever and unto ages of ages.' In a
voice soft and reassured the deacon says, 'Amen', and goes
out of the sanctuary by the north door to the people. Standing before the Royal Gates, he repeats once more within
himself: 'O Lord, open thou my lips; and my mouth shall
shew forth thy praise' (*Ps. li*, 15), and turning towards the
sanctuary calls again upon the priest to bid a blessing. From
within the holy place the priest answers: 'Blessed is the
kingdom . . .' and the Liturgy begins.

ii

THE LITURGY
OF THE CATECHUMENS

THE second part of the Liturgy is called the Liturgy of the Catechumens. Just as the first part, the Offertory, corresponds to the early life of Christ (to His Nativity which was revealed only to the angels and a handful of men, to His childhood and the hidden years in obscurity) until the time came for Him to appear in the world—so the second part answers to His life among men whom He instructed in the word of truth. It is also called the Liturgy of the Catechumens because during the first centuries of Christianity those who were only preparing to become Christians, those who had not yet received holy baptism and were still catechumens, were admitted to it. Moreover, the very form of the service, consisting of readings from the prophets, the Epistle and the Gospel, is pre-eminently catechistical.

The priest begins the Liturgy by proclaiming in a loud voice from the depths of the sanctuary: *Blessed is the Kingdom of the Father, and of the Son, and of the Holy Spirit.* . . . As by the Incarnation of the Son the mystery of the Trinity became manifest to the world, so therefore does this ascription to the Trinity precede and illumine the commencement of each action, and the worshipper, detaching himself from all else, should from the first summons rise in thought to the kingdom of the Trinity.

The deacon, standing before the Royal Gates like an angel urging the people to prayer, with three fingers of his right hand raises his stole—in the likeness of an angel's wing—and calls on the congregation to join in the prayers which the Church has prayed, unchanged since the time of the Apostles, beginning with the supplication for peace, without which it is impossible to pray. The assembled worshippers, making the sign of the cross over themselves, and striving to turn their hearts into stringed instruments tuned and responsive to every exhortation of the deacon, echo the choir: *Lord, have mercy!*

Standing before the ikonostasis, holding his prayer-stole like the lifted wing of an angel, and urging the people to prayer, the deacon prays: for peace from on high and for the salvation of our souls; for the peace of the whole world; for the good estate of the holy Churches of God and for the union of all; for this holy temple and those who with faith, reverence and godly fear enter therein; for our patriarch, for our bishop and rulers spiritual and temporal, for the courts of justice, the armed forces, for this city and the monastery or church in which the Liturgy is being celebrated, for every city and land and for those who with faith dwell therein; for fair seasons, for an abundance of the fruits of the earth, for peace in our time; for all who travel by land or by water, for the sick and suffering, for those in captivity and for their salvation; and that we may be delivered from all tribulation, wrath and necessity. To each of these various intercessions, which are gathered into an all-embracing chain of supplication called the Greater Litany, the congregation exclaims (in spirit) with the choir: *Lord, have mercy!*

In token of the impotence of our prayers which lack

spiritual purity and celestial force, the deacon, mindful of those who knew better than we do how to pray, calls on us to give ourselves and one another and our whole life to Christ our God. Sincerely desiring so to give ourselves and one another and our whole life to Christ our God, like the Mother of God and the saints and all those more holy than we are, the whole church exclaims with the choir: *To Thee, O Lord!* The priest completes the chain of supplication with the lesser doxology which like a uniting thread runs through the whole Liturgy, beginning and ending its every act. The choir (for the congregation) responds with a confirmatory *Amen*—so be it, so be it! After this comes the chanting of the antiphons.

The antiphons are versicles taken from the Psalms, prophetically proclaiming the coming of the Son of God into the world, and are sung in turn by the choir on either side. They take the place of the Psalms, which used to be sung in a fuller form.

During the singing of the first antiphon the priest prays secretly within the sanctuary, while the deacon stands in an attitude of prayer before the ikon of the Saviour, holding up his prayer-stole with three fingers. But at the end of the first antiphon he returns to the tribune[1] and calls upon the congregation with the words: *Again and again in peace let us pray unto the Lord!* The assembly of worshippers responds *Lord, have mercy!* Looking at the faces of the saints on the ikonostasis, the deacon exhorts the congregation anew to remembrance of the Mother of God and all the saints, and to the offering of themselves and one another, and of their whole lives to Christ the Lord. The choir, in the name of all the worshippers, responds *To Thee, O Lord!*

[1] *Amvon*, or tribune: the place immediately in front of the Royal Gates. [*Tr.*]

The priest closes with the *Gloria Patri*. The whole church utters a corroborative *Amen*. The chanting of the second antiphon follows.

During the second antiphon the priest in the sanctuary prays silently. The deacon stands in an attitude of prayer before the ikon of the Saviour, holding up his prayer-stole with three fingers. At the end he returns once more to the tribune and, looking on the countenances of the saints, summons the faithful to prayer as before: *In peace let us pray unto the Lord!* The choir answers for the people with *Lord, have mercy!* The deacon prays: *Defend, spare, save and preserve us, O God, by Thy grace.* The congregation echoes the choir's *Lord, have mercy!* Lifting his eyes to the countenances of the saints, the deacon continues: *Mindful of our most holy and undefiled, most blessed and glorious Lady, Mary ever Virgin and Mother of God, and all the saints, let us commend ourselves, and one another, and our whole life to Christ our God.* The congregation responds *To Thee, O Lord!* The litany ends with the doxology, to which the whole church responds with the affirming *Amen*, and the deacon departs into the sanctuary, where the priest prays secretly in these words: 'O Thou Who hast given us grace at this time with one accord to make our common supplications unto Thee, and dost promise, that when two or three are gathered together in Thy Name Thou wilt grant their requests: Fulfil now, O Lord, the desires and petitions of Thy servants, as may be most expedient for them, granting us in this world knowledge of Thy truth, and in the world to come life everlasting.'

From the choir, for everyone to hear, ring out the Beatitudes, proclaiming in this world knowledge of truth and in the world to come life everlasting. The congregation,

c

echoing the cry of the wise thief to Christ upon the Cross, 'Remember us, O Lord, when Thou comest into Thy kingdom' [cf. *Luke xxiii*, 42], repeats after the choir these words of the Saviour:

Blessed are the poor in spirit—those who are not proud or puffed up—*for theirs is the kingdom of heaven.*

Blessed are they that mourn—they that weep more bitterly over their own imperfections and transgressions than over the injuries and affronts they suffer from others—*for they shall be comforted.*

Blessed are the meek—those who do not nourish anger against anyone, who are forgiving and loving, and whose weapon is an all-conquering gentleness—*for they shall inherit the earth.*

Blessed are they which do hunger and thirst after righteousness—they who hunger for heavenly truth and thirst to establish it first and foremost in themselves—*for they shall be filled.*

Blessed are the merciful—they who feel pity for all men, and see Christ Himself pleading in everyone who asks for help—*for they shall obtain mercy.*

Blessed are the pure in heart: for they shall see God. Just as in the clear mirror of still waters, unclouded by mud or sand, the vault of heaven is reflected immaculate, so in the mirror of a pure heart, unsullied by the passions, nothing earthly remains, and the image of God alone is reflected in it.

Blessed are the peacemakers: for they shall be called the children of God. That is, they who bring peace and conciliation into the home are true sons of God (like the Son of God Himself Who came down upon earth in order to bring peace into our souls).

*Blessed are they which are persecuted for righteousness'
sake*—those who are persecuted for preaching the truth not
only with their lips but by the fragrance of their whole
lives—*for theirs is the kingdom of heaven.*

*Blessed are ye, when men shall revile you, and persecute you,
and shall say all manner of evil against you falsely, for my
sake. Rejoice, and be exceeding glad: for great is your reward
(Matt. v. 3-12)*—great, for their merits are threefold: first,
that in themselves they were spotless and pure; second, that
being pure they were reviled; third, that being reviled they
rejoiced to suffer for Christ.

The congregation of the faithful feelingly repeats after
the choir these words of the Saviour which declare those
who may await and hope for eternal life in the world to
come, who are the true kings of peace, the co-heirs and
participators in the heavenly kingdom.

Now the Royal Gates are solemnly opened, as though
they were the gates of the Kingdom of Heaven itself opening
wide, and before the eyes of the worshippers the altar,
radiant, stands revealed, like the habitation of the glory of
God and the seat of heavenly wisdom whence flows out to
us knowledge of truth and the proclamation of eternal life.
Approaching the altar, the priest and the deacon take from
it the book of the Gospels and carry it forth to the people,
not by way of the Royal Gates but passing behind the holy
table and going out through the side-door in memory of
the door of the side-room through which, in primitive times,
books were carried into the centre of the church to be read.

The faithful look upon the book of the Gospels, carried
in the hands of the humble ministers of the church, as upon
the Saviour Himself coming forth for the first time for the
work of divine preaching: He comes through the narrow

north door, as it were unknown, into the midst of the
temple, in order, having appeared to all, to return to the
sanctuary by way of the Royal Gates. God's servitors halt
in the middle of the church. Both bow their heads. The
priest prays silently that He Who stablished in heaven the
ranks of angels and archangels to minister to His glory shall
now bid these same powers and spirits who serve with us
to accomplish together with us the entrance into the holy
place; and the deacon, indicating the Royal Gates with his
prayer-stole, says to him: *Bless, O master, the holy entrance.*
To which the priest returns: *Blessed is the entrance of Thy
holy things always, now and for ever, and in all eternity.*
Having held the book of the Gospels for the priest to kiss,
the deacon carries it into the sanctuary, but pauses between
the Royal Gates and, raising it in his hands, cries: *All-
Wisdom!* in token that the Word of God, His Son, His
eternal wisdom was made known to the world through the
Gospels which he now holds aloft. And immediately after
he cries: *Stand erect and steadfast!*—that is, rouse yourselves
from your inertness, your careless inattention.

The congregation, lifting up their hearts, echo the choir:
*O come, let us worship and fall down before Christ. Save us,
O Son of God, who sing unto Thee: Alleluia!* (The Hebrew
word 'Alleluia' means 'The Lord cometh, praise the Lord!'
But since, according to the essence of Holy Writ, both the
present and the future are contained in the word 'cometh'—
He cometh Who is come and Who draweth near again—so,
signifying the eternal coming of God, this word 'Alleluia'
is heard during the celebration every time the Lord Himself
comes forth to the people in the guise of the Gospels or
the sacred Gifts.)

The book of the Gospels, which proclaims the word of

life, is laid upon the altar. The choir sings either the anthem in honour of the festival of the day or a troparion or hymn in praise of the saint whom the Church is honouring that day; honouring for that he resembled those whom Christ spoke of in the Beatitudes which we have just heard and who by his own life showed us how to rise after Christ into life eternal.

The troparion is followed by the singing of the trisagion. Having asked the priest's blessing on the hymn, the deacon appears between the Royal Gates and, lifting his orarion, gives the sign to the choir. Triumphantly the trisagion, the threefold cry to God—*O Holy God, O Holy and Mighty One, O Holy and Immortal, have mercy upon us*—rings out through the church. By the invocation 'O Holy God' the trisagion proclaims God the Father. 'Holy and Mighty' proclaims God the Son, His strength, His creative Word. The invocation to the 'Holy and Immortal One' proclaims His immortal providence, the eternally living will of God— the Holy Spirit.

Thrice the choir repeats the hymn, that all may hear how in the eternal abiding of God there abode in Him the eternal abiding of the Trinity, and at no time did God exist without the Word, or the Word without the Holy Spirit. 'By the word of the Lord were the heavens made, and all the host of them by the breath of his mouth,' says the Psalmist. (*Ps. xxxiii*, 6.) Each of the faithful knows that as one in the likeness of God he too possesses this same trebleness: in him are God Himself, His word and His Spirit, or thought which gives birth to the word, but he realises that his human word is without power, is spoken in vain and creates nothing, while his spirit does not belong to him, influenced as he is by every casual impression—it is only when his whole self has been

lifted up to God that word and spirit acquire strength. Then
his word is a reflection of God's word, his spirit of God's
Spirit, and the image of the creating Trinity is sealed in the
creature, and the creature becomes in the likeness of the
Creator. Recognising all this, each of the faithful, listening
to the trisagion, prays within himself that God the Holy,
Strong and Immortal One, having cleansed him throughly,
should adopt him for His temple and abode; and three times
he repeats within himself: 'O Holy God, O Holy and
Mighty One, O Holy and Immortal, have mercy upon us!'

The priest secretly within the sanctuary prays for the
acceptance of the trisagion, prostrates himself thrice before
the altar and thrice repeats to himself 'O Holy God, O Holy
and Mighty One, O Holy and Immortal!' And similarly the
deacon thrice repeats to himself the hymn of the trisagion
and like the priest thrice bows before the holy altar.

After the threefold reverence the priest retires to the high
place, as into the depth of the knowledge of God, whence
flowed forth to us the mystery of the Most Holy Trinity;
he retires as into that most exalted and all-embracing of
places, where the Son abides in the bosom of the Father in
the unity of the Holy Spirit. And by his going into the high
place the priest symbolises the ascension of Christ Himself
in the flesh into the bosom of the Father summoning man
to follow after into the Father's bosom—the new birth seen
from afar by the prophet Daniel, who dreamed in his vision
of how the Son of man came even to the Ancient of days.
[cf. *Dan. vii*, 13.] With a firm step the priest goes, saying
the while: 'Blessed is he that cometh in the name of the
Lord' (*Matt. xxi*, 9), and at the deacon's invocation to
'Bless, Father, the throne on high' he gives his blessing
with the words 'Blessed art Thou upon the glorious throne

of Thy kingdom, Who sittest upon the Cherubim, now and for ever and unto ages of ages.' And the priest seats himself in the high place beside the throne which is reserved for the bishop. Thence, as an apostle of God and his vicar, with his face turned towards the people, he prepares to listen to the reading of the Apostolic epistle. He listens seated to show that he is equal with the apostles.

The reader, holding the book of the Epistles in his hand, advances to the centre of the church. The deacon calls for the attention of all present: *Let us give heed*. The priest from the depths of the sanctuary sends reader and congregation the salutation of peace. The congregation responds likewise to the priest. But as his office must be a spiritual one, like the office of the apostles, who spoke not their own words but whose lips were moved by the Holy Spirit, they reply not 'Peace be with thee', but *And with thy spirit*. The deacon cries *Wisdom!* Loudly and expressively, that each word may be heard by all, the reader begins. Diligently, with receptive hearts, with questing soul, and mind probing the inner meaning of what is being read, the congregation attends, for the reading of the Epistle serves as a step or ladder towards a better understanding of the reading of the Gospel. When the reader comes to the end the priest exclaims from the sanctuary *Peace be with thee!* The reader responds *And with thy spirit*. The deacon exclaims *Wisdom!* From the choir sounds the *Alleluia*, announcing the approach of the Lord coming to speak to the people through the words of the Gospel.

With the censer the deacon fills the church with fragrance for the reception of the Lord, reminding us by his censing of the purity of soul with which we should attend to the fragrant words of the Gospel. The priest in the sanctuary prays secretly that the light of Divine wisdom may shine into our hearts, and that our minds be opened to understanding of the preaching of the Gospel. For the shining of that light into their hearts the congregation prays inwardly, while preparing to listen. Having asked the blessing of the priest, and receiving from him the commendation 'May God, through the intercessions of the most holy and all-laudable Apostle and Evangelist N. grant utterance with great power unto thee who proclaimest the good tidings, unto the fulfilling of the Gospel of His well-beloved Son, our Lord Jesus Christ', the deacon steps forth to the tribune, preceded by a tall candle which is carried before him and signifies the all-illuminating light of Christ. The priest in the sanctuary exclaims *Wisdom! Stand steadfast. Let us hear the holy Gospel. Peace be with you all.* The choir responds *And with thy spirit.* The deacon begins the reading.

With heads bowed in reverence, listening as it were to Christ Himself speaking from the tribune, the faithful strive to receive into their hearts the seed of the holy Word which the heavenly Sower Himself sows by the mouth of His minister—not into hearts likened by the Saviour to the earth by the wayside, on which, though the seed fall, yet it is straightway devoured by the birds of the air—by evil thoughts which swoop down; not into hearts which He likened to stony ground having no depth of earth—hearts which, though they receive the Word with gladness, do not permit of Its taking deep root because they have no depth; neither into hearts which He likens to ground which is all thorns, where, though the seed spring up, yet it is soon choked by the thorns which grow up with it—the cares and troubles of this world, the manifold distractions of this earthly, mortal life with its deceiving pleasures which overwhelm the young shoots so that the seed remains without fruit; but into receptive hearts which He likens to good ground bringing forth fruit, some an hundredfold, some sixty, some thirty—the hearts of those who, when they have gone home from church, tend what they have received, among their families, at their work, in leisure, in conversation and in solitude. In short, each of the faithful strives to be both the hearer and the doer whom the Saviour likens to the wise man who builds his house not upon the sand but upon a rock, so that though, on leaving the church, the rains, floods and tempests of every disaster should fall on him his spiritual house stands firm as a fortress upon a rock. At the end of the reading the priest from the sanctuary proclaims to the deacon: *Peace be with thee, that bringest good tidings.* Lifting their heads, all those present in thankfulness of heart echo the choir's *Glory to Thee, O God. Glory to Thee.* Standing between the Royal Gates, the priest receives the book of the Gospels from the deacon and places it upon the altar, even as the Word having come forth from God and being returned to Him. The sanctuary, representing the heavenly places on high, is now hidden from sight—the Royal Gates are closed, the curtain is drawn, signifying that there is no other door into the Kingdom of Heaven save that opened by Christ. Only with Him may one enter in: 'I am the door.' (*John x*, 9.)

In early Christian times it was usual at this point to have the sermon: the explanation and interpretation of the foregoing passage from the Gospel. But as in our day the sermon is more generally preached on other texts, and therefore does not take the form of a commentary on the Gospel, it has been transferred to the end of the service so as not to break the ordered sequence of the Liturgy.

Like an angel inspiring the people to prayer, the deacon goes to the tribune to call on the congregation to pray still more ardently and assiduously. *Let us all say—with all our soul, with all our mind let us say*: he exclaims, with three fingers raising his prayer-stole; and in the name of the congregation the choir, in burning supplication, responds *Lord, have mercy!* Intensifying the prayer by a threefold petition for mercy, the deacon again exhorts us to pray for all men of whatever rank or calling, beginning with those in the highest places, where responsibility lies heavier, where stumbling blocks are bigger and the need of God's help is greater. All present, knowing how much the welfare of the many depends upon the just fulfilment of their duties by those in authority, pray that God may enlighten them to the proper execution of their functions and grant to each the strength to tread the course of his earthly life with honour. For this the congregation prays with especial diligence, exclaiming not once but three times *Lord, have mercy!* The whole chain of these supplications is called the Greater Litany, or Litany of Fervent Supplication, and the priest within the sanctuary, before the altar, prays with all his heart for the acceptance of this devout supplication in a prayer which is actually called the Prayer of Fervent Supplication.

And if on this day there be any offering made for the dead, then immediately after the Greater Litany comes the Litany for those who have departed this life. Holding his orarion with three fingers, the deacon calls upon the congregation to pray for the repose of the souls of the servants of God, whom he names, that God may grant them forgiveness for their every transgression, voluntary and involuntary, and bring their souls to rest where the righteous rest. Everyone present here recalls to memory all those dear to him who have fallen asleep, and after every petition repeats thrice to himself the deacon's *Lord, have mercy*, praying devoutly both for his own dead and for all departed Christians. *For the mercy of God, the kingdom of heaven, and the remission of their sins, let us beseech Christ, our Immortal King and God*, exclaims the deacon. The congregation responds mentally with the choir which sings *Grant, O Lord*. Thereupon the priest within the sanctuary prays that He Who hath overcome death and given life unto the world should give rest to the souls of His departed servants in a green place, in a quiet place, from whence pain, sorrow and sighing are fled away; and, having silently asked for forgiveness for them for all their sins, says aloud: *For Thou art the Resurrection, and the Life, and the Repose of Thy departed servants, O Christ, our God, and unto Thee we ascribe glory together with Thine unbegotten Father, and Thy most holy and good and life-giving Spirit, now and for ever and unto ages of ages*. The choir responds with a positive *Amen*. The deacon begins the litany for the catechumens.

Although nowadays there be few persons who have not been baptised and so are under instruction, yet each one present, reflecting how far in faith and works he is from the believers in the early days of Christianity who were found worthy to be present at the feast of love; realising how he, so to speak, is only taught of Christ but has not taken Him into the core of his life; only hears His words with his mind but does not put them into effect, his faith still cold, and the fire of all-forgiving love to his brother, which melts the hardness of the soul, still wanting; reflecting that, baptised by water in the name of Christ, he has not attained regeneration in the spirit, without which his Christianity is nothing worth, according to the words of the Saviour himself:

'Except a man be born from above, he cannot enter into the heavenly kingdom' [cf. *John iii*, 5]—thinking on all these things, each of those present contritely places himself among the number of the catechumens, and at the call of the deacon, *Catechumens, pray ye to the Lord*, from the depths of his heart responds *Lord, have mercy!*

Ye faithful, cries the deacon, *let us pray for the catechumens, that the Lord may have mercy upon them; may instruct them in the word of truth; reveal unto them the Gospel of righteousness; unite them to His Holy, Catholick, and Apostolick Church; that He may save them, have mercy upon them, protect and preserve them by His grace.*

And the faithful, feeling how little worthy they are to be so called, while they pray for the catechumens pray also for themselves, and to each separate invocation of the deacon silently repeat after the choir: *Lord, have mercy*. The deacon summons the catechumens to bow their heads unto the Lord. All bow their heads, saying inwardly *To Thee, O Lord*.

The priest meanwhile prays in secret for the catechumens and for those who in humility of spirit have placed themselves among the catechumens. 'O Lord our God, Who dwellest on high, Who dost behold the humble, Who for the salvation of mankind didst send forth Thy Son, our God and our Lord, look down upon Thy servants the catechumens, who have bowed their necks before Thee. Unite them to Thy Church, and number them among Thy chosen flock.' [And aloud] *That they also with us may glorify Thy most honourable and majestic Name, Father, Son and Holy Spirit, now and for ever and unto ages of ages.* The choir sounds the *Amen*. And as a reminder that the moment has come when, in olden times, the catechumens were led out of the church the deacon cries in a loud voice *Ye catechumens, depart!* And again, more loudly, *Ye catechumens, depart!* And then a third time: *Ye catechumens, depart! Let none of the catechumens but only the faithful remain; again and again, in peace let us pray to the Lord.*

At these words do all tremble who feel their unworthiness. Crying in thought to Christ Himself, Who drove out of the temple of God the sellers and shameless hucksters who turned His holy house into a market-place, each one present strives to drive from the temple of his soul the carnal man, the catechumen unfit to be present at the holy act, and beseeches Christ Himself to set up in him a faithful heart and count him among the chosen flock, of whom the Apostle said 'a holy nation, a peculiar people, stones building up a spiritual house' [cf. 1 *Peter ii*, 5]—that Christ may reckon him among the true believers who were present at the Liturgy in the first centuries of Christianity, whose countenances now look upon him from the ikonostasis. And running his gaze over them all, he calls upon them for help, as brethren praying now in heaven, for the most holy acts are about to take place—the Liturgy of the Faithful begins.

iii

THE LITURGY
OF THE FAITHFUL

WITHIN the closed sanctuary the priest spreads on the altar the corporal—a cloth bearing a representation of the body of the Saviour. Upon this cloth he will place the holy bread, prepared by him during the Offertory, and cup of wine and water, which are now brought with solemn ceremony from the small side altar, in the sight of all the faithful. The corporal recalls the time when Christians were persecuted, and the Church had no settled abode. They could not carry an altar from place to place, so they used a communion cloth into which relics of saints were sewn. To us in our day the corporal proclaims that the Church is not confined to any exclusive building, city or locality but rides like a ship on the waves of this world, nowhere coming to anchor, for her anchor is cast in heaven. Having spread out the corporal, the officiating priest approaches the altar as it were for the first time, as though he were only now preparing to begin the actual service, for in the primitive Church it was only at this point that the altar was revealed to the congregation. Until now, because of the presence of the catechumens, it had been curtained off and hidden. Only now begins the real supplication of the faithful. Still within the closed sanctuary the priest prostrates himself before the altar, and in the first and second Prayers of the Faithful he prays for his own purifying, that he may stand uncondemned before the holy altar, and be made worthy to offer the sacrifice with the testimony of a pure conscience. Meanwhile the deacon, standing on the tribune in the middle of the church like an angel exhorting to prayer, his orarion lifted and held with three fingers, calls upon the faithful to repeat the same supplications with which the Liturgy of the Catechumens began.

And striving as before to attune their hearts to the harmony of peace, now ever more instant, all the faithful exclaim: *Lord, have mercy!* and pray still more fervently for the peace which is from above, and for the salvation of our souls, for the peace of the whole world, for the good estate of the Churches of God and the union of all, for this holy temple and those who enter therein with faith, reverence and godly fear, that they may be delivered from all affliction, wrath and necessity; crying ever the more earnestly in their hearts: 'Lord, have mercy!'

The priest from the depths of the sanctuary proclaims *Wisdom*, signifying that the same Wisdom, the same Eternal Son of God Who came forth in the guise of the Gospel to sow the Word of Life, will now be brought forth in the form of the holy Bread and offered in sacrifice for the whole world. Moved by this reminder, the worshippers turn their thoughts to the approaching solemn sacerdotal act, while the priest silently recites this noble prayer: 'None is worthy among them that are bound with fleshly desires and pleasures to approach Thee, or draw nigh and serve Thee, O King of Glory; for to minister unto Thee is a great and terrible thing, even for the heavenly powers themselves.

But forasmuch as in Thine immeasurable love Thou didst become Man, suffering thereby no change or alteration, and art Thyself made an high priest for us, and Thyself didst bestow on us the performance of this divine office, of this unbloody sacrifice, as Lord of all—for Thou only, O God, hast dominion over heaven and earth, Who art borne by Cherubim upon the throne, Lord of the Seraphim and King of Israel, Thou only art holy and dost repose in the saints— I make my supplication unto Thee Who alone art good: Look down upon me, Thy sinful and unprofitable servant, and cleanse my soul and my heart from an evil conscience, and by the power of Thy Holy Spirit enable me who am invested with the grace of the priesthood to stand before this Thy holy table and to sacrifice Thy most pure and sacred Body and Thy precious Blood. For unto Thee I come, to Thee I bow my head and make my prayer before Thee: Turn not Thy Face from me, neither cast me from among Thy children; but vouchsafe to accept these gifts from me, Thine unworthy servant; for Thou art both He that offerest and art offered, Thou dost receive and art given, O Christ our God, and unto Thee we ascribe glory together with Thy Father, Who is without beginning, and Thy most holy, gracious and life-giving Spirit, now and for ever and unto ages of ages.'

The Royal Gates are opened during this prayer, to reveal the celebrant praying with outstretched arms. The deacon, with the censer in his hand, comes forth to prepare the way for the King of all, and—by an abundance of incense which rises in a cloud of fragrance in the midst of which is He Who is borne by the Cherubim—reminds the congregation that they should direct their prayer like incense unto the Lord; to remember that, being in the words of the Apostle a 'sweet savour of Christ' (2 *Cor. ii*, 15), they should be pure as cherubim in order to receive the Lord. And the choirs on either side, in the name of the whole church, begin the Cherubical hymn: *Let us, the Cherubim mystically representing, and unto the life-giving Trinity the thrice-holy chant intoning, now lay aside all earthly care; that we may raise on high the King of all, by the angelic hosts invisibly attended. Allelulia, Alleluia, Alleluia.*

It was the custom among the ancient Romans for the newly chosen emperor to be borne out to the people, escorted by his warriors, on a shield and under an archway of a multitude of spears inclined before him. The hymn was composed by one of these emperors, who, his own earthly grandeur withal, bowed to the ground before the grandeur and majesty of the King of all, now borne forth by the Cherubim and the legions of the heavenly host. The emperors of old used to station themselves humbly among the officiating clergy when the sacred Bread was carried forth.

The final Alleluia is the actual Cherubical hymn, as chanted by the invisible powers in the heights. Repeating it inwardly to themselves, priest and deacon approach the small side altar where the Offertory was performed. Going to the gifts, which are covered with the *aer*, the deacon says, 'Take, master!' The priest removes the *aer* and lays it on the deacon's left shoulder, saying, 'Lift up your hands in the sanctuary, and bless the Lord.' (*Ps. cxxxiv*, 2.) Then he takes the paten with the Lamb and places it on the deacon's head, and himself takes the holy chalice, and, preceded by a candle or a lamp, they go forth through the north door to the people. If the service is in a cathedral, with a number of priests and deacons celebrating, one carries the paten,

D

another the chalice, a third the spoon with which the faithful are communicated, a fourth the spear which pierced the Sacred Body. All the objects used during the holy sacrifice are brought forth, even the sponge with which the crumbs of holy bread are gathered on the paten, and which represents the sponge filled with vinegar that men gave their Creator to drink. [cf. *Matt. xxvii*, 48.] To the singing of the Cherubical hymn the solemn procession appears, like a procession of the heavenly powers. It is called the Great Entrance.

At the sight of the King of all, carried in the humble guise of the Lamb lying on the paten, as on a shield, surrounded by the instruments of His earthly Passion, like the spears of the innumerable heavenly host all bow their heads and pray in the words of the thief on the cross: 'Lord, remember me when thou comest into thy kingdom.' (*Luke xxiii*, 42.) The procession pauses in the midst of the temple. The priest makes use of this great moment to remember before the Lord, in the presence of the gifts he bears, all Christian men, beginning with those whose obligations are the heaviest and most sacred, upon the fulfilment of which depend the welfare of all and the very salvation of their souls, and ending with the words: *You and all Orthodox Christians—may the Lord God remember you in His kingdom, now and for ever and unto ages of ages.* The choir concludes the Cherubical hymn with the thrice-repeated chant of *Alleluia*, announcing the eternal progress of the Lord. The procession makes its way through the Royal Gates. Entering the sanctuary first, the deacon, standing on the right side of the Gates, meets the priest with the words: 'May the Lord God remember thy sacred ministry in His kingdom', to which the priest replies: 'May the Lord God remembethy holy diaconate in His kingdom, now and for ever and unto ages of ages.' And he lays the sacred chalice and the bread representing the Body of Christ on the altar as in a grave. The Royal Gates are closed, like the doors of the tomb closing on the Lord; the curtain above them is drawn, custodian, as it were, set on guard before the tomb. The priest takes the sacred paten from the deacon's head, as though he were lifting the Body of Christ from the Cross, and lays it on the outspread corporal as upon a winding sheet, saying as he does so: 'Down from the tree Joseph, "a good man, and a just", took Thy most pure Body and, wrapping it in a clean linen cloth with spices, laid it in a new sepulchre.' [cf. *Luke xxiii*, 53; *John xix*, 40, 41.] And remembering the omnipresence of Him Who now lies before him in the grave, he repeats silently: 'In the grave wast Thou in the flesh, in the spirit didst Thou descend into hell, as God wast Thou in paradise with the thief, and withal wast Thou on the throne with the Father and the Spirit— Christ indescribable, Who dost fulfil all things.' Remembering the glory with which the sepulchre was filled, he says: 'Thy life-giving tomb is revealed to us lovelier far than paradise, more radiant than a king's palace, O Christ, Fountain of our resurrection.' And taking the veil from the paten and the chalice, and from the deacon's shoulder the *aer*, which now represents, not the swaddling-clothes in which the Infant Jesus was wrapped, but the winding-sheet round His dead Body, he censes them and covers the paten and the chalice with them again, saying: 'Down from the tree Joseph, "a good man, and a just", took Thy most pure Body and, wrapping it in a clean linen cloth with spices, laid it in a new sepulchre.' Then, receiving the censer from the deacon, he censes the holy gifts, bowing thrice before them, and, in preparation for the coming oblation, silently repeats the words of the prophet David: 'Do good in thy good pleasure unto Zion: build thou the walls of Jerusalem. Then shalt thou be pleased with the sacrifice of righteousness, with burnt offering and whole burnt offering: then shall they offer bullocks upon thine altar.' (*Ps. li*, 18.) For except God Himself build the walls of Jerusalem to guard our souls from all carnal devices we are not able to offer Him sacrifice or burnt offering, nor can the flame of our inward supplication rise on high, blown about as it is by irrelevant thoughts, onslaughts of the passions, and the buffetings of inner turmoil. Praying that he may be cleansed for the approaching sacrifice, the priest returns the censer to the deacon and letting his vestment fall over his arms he bows his head and says: 'Remember me, brother and fellow minister.'—'The Lord God remember thy sacred ministry in His Kingdom,' replies the deacon, and in his turn, reflecting on his own unworthiness, he bows his head and, holding up his orarion with three fingers of his right hand, says: 'Pray for me, holy master.' The priest responds: 'The Holy Ghost shall come upon thee, and the power of the Highest shall overshadow thee.' (*Luke i*, 35.) 'The same Spirit shall labour with us all the days of our life,' answers the deacon. And, filled with the consciousness of his unworthiness, he continues: 'Remember me, holy father.' The priest replies, 'The Lord God remember thee in His kingdom, always, now and for ever and unto ages of ages.' The deacon exclaims 'Amen!' and, having kissed the priest's hand, he goes out at the north door to call upon all present to pray for the holy gifts that have been brought forth and placed upon the altar.

Standing on the tribune, facing the Royal Gates, holding

up his orarion with the three fingers of the right hand, like the uplifted wing of an angel urging to prayer, the deacon offers a litany of supplications which differ from those of the former litanies. Beginning with the exhortation to pray for the gifts which have been brought to the altar, he quickly passes on to petitions such as only the faithful dwelling in Christ can make to the Lord.

That this whole day may be perfect, holy, peaceful and without sin, we beseech the Lord, invokes the deacon. The congregation of worshippers, in unison with the choir, echo in their hearts: *We beseech Thee, O Lord.*

For an angel of peace, faithful guide and guardian of our souls, we beseech the Lord.

Those present: *Grant us, O Lord.*

For pardon and remission of our sins and transgressions, we beseech the Lord.

Those present: *Grant us, O Lord.*

For all things good and profitable to our souls, and peace for the world, we beseech the Lord.

Those present: *Grant us, O Lord.*

That we may pass the remainder of our lives in peace and repentance, we beseech the Lord.

Those present: *Grant us, O Lord.*

For a Christian ending to our life, painless, without shame and peaceful, and a good defence before the dread judgment-seat of Christ, we beseech Thee.

Those present: *Grant us, O Lord.*

Calling to remembrance our most holy, most pure, most blessed and glorious Lady and Mother of God, together with all the saints, let us commend ourselves and one another and all our life to Christ our God.

And in a sincere desire thus to commend themselves and

one another to Christ the Lord, all cry: *To Thee, O Lord!*

The litany concludes with the exclamation: *Through the bountiful mercies of Thine only-begotten Son, with Whom Thou art blessed, together with Thy most holy, good and life-giving Spirit, now and for ever and unto ages of ages.*

Amen, chants the choir.

The sanctuary is still closed. The priest has not yet begun the offering of the sacrifice: much has still to come before the sacramental supper. From the depths of the sanctuary he proclaims the salutation of the Saviour Himself: *Peace be unto you.* (*Luke xxiv*, 36; *John xx*, 19.) *And with thy spirit*, answers the congregation. Standing on the tribune, the deacon, as in the time of the early Christians, exhorts all present to mutual love, saying, *Let us love one another that with one mind we may confess.* . . . The choir takes up and concludes the appeal with the words: . . . *the Father, and the Son, and the Holy Spirit, Trinity consubstantial and undivided*; for without love for one another we cannot love Him Who is love, perfect and complete, embracing in His Trinity the loving and the loved, and the very love with which the one loves the other: the One Who loves is God the Father; the One Who is loved is God the Son, and the Love which unites Them is God the Holy Spirit. Thrice the priest makes obeisance in the sanctuary, as he repeats silently: 'I will love thee, O Lord, my strength. The Lord is my rock, and my fortress' (*Ps. xviii*, 1), and kisses the holy paten and chalice covered by the veil, and the edge of the holy table; and however many priests are serving with him, each of them does the same, after which they kiss one another on the shoulder. The senior priest says: 'Christ is in the midst of us', and the others respond, 'He is and shall be.' In like manner the deacons, as many as be present, kiss each the cross upon his stole, and then each other's shoulder, while repeating the words used by the priests.

In former times all who were present in the church kissed one another—men kissing men, and women exchanging the kiss of peace with women, some saying, 'Christ is in the midst of us', while others answered, 'He is and shall be.' Therefore now, too, each present, calling to mind all Christians, not only those in church with him but those who are absent; not only those who are dear to him but those estranged from him, and hastening to be reconciled towards those for whom he has felt dislike, hatred or displeasure— he embraces them all in thought, repeating inwardly, 'Christ is in the midst of us', and answering in their name, 'He is and shall be.' Otherwise—without this—he will be dead to all that follows. Christ bade us 'Leave there thy gift before the altar, and go thy way; first be reconciled to thy brother, and then come and offer thy gift.' (*Matt. v*, 24.) Likewise, the Apostle of Christ declared, 'If a man say, "I love God", and hateth his brother, he is a liar: for he that loveth not his brother whom he hath seen, how can he love God whom he hath not seen?' (1 *John iv*, 20.)

Standing on the tribune with his face towards the faithful and holding his orarion with three fingers, the deacon pronounces the ancient warning: *The doors! The doors!* which in former days was addressed to the janitors standing by the doors into the church, that they let none enter who might disturb the rite of Christian worship or profane the temple. Today the words are addressed to the worshippers themselves, admonishing them to guard the doors of their hearts, now become the abode of love, lest any enemy of love break in, and to look to it that their mouths and ears be opened to the recitation of the Creed, in token of which the curtain is drawn back from the Royal Gates—the heavenly gates which are opened only when it is meet and proper to fix the attention on the highest mysteries. With the words *In wisdom let us give heed* the deacon calls upon the congregation to listen to the Creed. In firm, resolute tones, declaiming rather than singing, the choir loudly and expressively recites the Creed. *I believe in one God the Father Almighty, Maker of heaven and earth, And of all things visible and invisible.* . . . After the briefest of pauses to allow the thoughts of all to rest on the First Person of the Holy Trinity—God the Father—the choir continues in a higher key: *And in one Lord Jesus Christ, the only-begotten Son of God, Begotten of his Father before all worlds, Light of Light, Very God of very God, Begotten, not made, Being of one substance with the Father, By whom all things were made: Who for us men and for our salvation came down from heaven, And was incarnate by the Holy Ghost of the Virgin Mary, And was made man, And was crucified also for us under Pontius Pilate. He suffered and was buried, And the third day he rose again according to the Scriptures, And ascended into heaven, And sitteth on the right hand of the Father. And he shall come again with glory to judge both the quick and the dead: Whose kingdom shall have no end. And I believe in the Holy Ghost, The Lord and giver of life, Who proceedeth from the Father, Who with the Father and the Son together is worshipped and glorified, Who spake by the Prophets.* After another instant's pause for our minds to dwell on the Third Person of the Holy Trinity—God the Holy Spirit—the singers resume: *In one Holy, Catholick and Apostolick Church. I acknowledge one Baptism for the remission of sins. And I look for the Resurrection of the dead, And the life of the world to come. Amen.*

In firm, resolute tones, impressing every word upon the heart, the choir chants this Creed, which the congregation repeats word for word. Taking courage in heart and spirit, the priest before the altar, symbol of the holy table of the Last Supper, silently repeats to himself the Creed, as do all serving with him, while they raise and lower, raise and lower, the holy *aer* over the sacred gifts.

And with resolute step the deacon comes forth and exclaims: *Let us be upright, let us stand with fear, let us take heed to present the holy offering in peace*—that is, Let us stand as it behoves man to stand before God, in fear and trembling, and yet with the brave confidence of the spirit that praises God with the recovered harmony of peace in the heart, without which it is impossible to aspire to God. In answer to the deacon's appeal the whole church, offering in sacrifice the praise of the lips and the unction of the heart, makes answer with the choir: *The oil of kindness, the sacrifice of praise.*[cf. *Ps. cxli*, 5.] In the primitive church it was the custom at this point to offer oil, in token of temper or disposition made soft and gentle. (The words for *oil* and *mercy* or *kindliness* are identical in the Greek language.)

Meanwhile, the priest within the sanctuary removes the veil from the holy gifts, kisses it and lays it aside, saying as he does so: 'The grace of our Lord . . .' The deacon, entering the sanctuary and taking in his hand the fan or *ripidion*, reverently fans the element.

Preparing to perform the Sacrament of the Lord's Supper, the priest from within the sanctuary sends the people the apostolic salutation: *The grace of our Lord Jesus Christ, and the love of God, and the communion of the Holy Ghost, be with you all.* (2 *Cor. xiii*, 13, 14.) To which the faithful respond *And with thy spirit.* And the sanctuary, which before represented the manger or cave, is now the upper room where the disciples made ready the passover. The altar, which represented the tomb, is no longer the grave but the table. In memory of the Saviour Who lifted up His eyes to heaven before giving the divine food to His disciples, the priest cries *Let us lift up our hearts!* And each one standing in the church reflects on what is about to be accomplished—that at this moment the Lamb of God is to be slain for him, the precious Blood of the Lord Himself is to be poured into the chalice for his cleansing, and all the heavenly powers are joining with the priest to pray for him. Thinking on all these things each turns his heart from earth to heaven, from darkness to light, and with his fellow-worshippers exclaims: *We lift them up unto the Lord.*

Remembering the Redeemer Who gave thanks,[1] the priest looks up to heaven and exclaims: *Let us give thanks unto the Lord.* The choir responds: *It is meet and right so to worship the Father, and the Son, and the Holy Spirit, the Trinity consubstantial and undivided.* And the priest prays secretly: 'It is meet and right to sing praises unto Thee, to bless Thee, to magnify Thee, to give thanks unto Thee, to worship Thee in all places under Thy dominion, for Thou art God, ineffable, unknowable, invisible, inconceivable, the same from everlasting to everlasting; Thou and Thine only-begotten Son and Thy Holy Spirit. Out of nothingness Thou hast brought us to being, and when we were fallen Thou didst raise us up again, and didst leave nothing undone till Thou hadst brought us to heaven, and hadst bestowed upon us Thy kingdom to come. For all these things we give thanks unto Thee, and to Thine only-begotten Son, and the Holy Spirit, for Thy benefits whereof we know and whereof

[1] [before the breaking of the bread at the holy supper. *Tr.*]

we know not, both manifest and concealed, which Thou has bestowed upon us. And we render thanks unto Thee for this ministry which thou has vouchsafed to receive at our hands, although before Thee stand hosts of archangels and tens of thousands of angels, the Cherubim and the many-eyed Seraphim that have six wings and soar aloft, singing, exclaiming and uttering the triumphal hymn: "Holy, holy, holy, Lord of Sabaoth; heaven and earth are full of Thy glory!" '

The whole choir of singers takes up this triumphant song of the seraphim, which the prophets heard in their holy visions. [cf. *Isa. vi*, 2.] The faithful lift their thoughts to the invisible heavens and together with the seraphim repeat, *Holy, holy, holy, Lord of Sabaoth*, with them surrounding the altar of divine glory. And as at this same moment the whole church awaits the descent of God Himself, coming to offer Himself in sacrifice for all, the hymn of the seraphim resounding in the heavens is completed by the song with which the Hebrew children met the Lord on His entry into Jerusalem, as they strewed branches in His path: *Hosanna; Blessed is he that cometh in the name of the Lord: Hosanna in the highest*. (*Mark xi*, 9.) For the Lord is about to enter the temple as into a mystic Jerusalem. The deacon continues to fan the holy gifts that no insect may settle thereon, and with his fanning symbolising the wafting of grace. Meanwhile the priest prays in secret: 'And we also, O Lord Who lovest mankind, in company with these blessed Powers, do cry aloud and say: Holy art Thou, Most Holy art Thou, and Thine only-begotten Son, and Thy Holy Spirit. Holy and most Holy art Thou, and great is the majesty of Thy glory, Who didst so love Thy world that Thou didst give Thine only-begotten Son, to the end that all that believe in Him should not perish, but have everlasting life (*John iii,* 16); Who being come and having accomplished all that was appointed for our sakes in the night that He was betrayed— nay, in the which He did give Himself for the life of the world—took bread in His holy and pure and spotless Hands, and when He had given thanks and blessed and hallowed it He brake it and gave it to His holy disciples and apostles, saying . . .' Here the priest utters aloud the words of the Saviour: *Take, eat; this is my Body which is broken for you for the remission of sins.* [cf. *Luke xxii,* 19, 20.] And the whole church echoes the choir's *Amen,* while the deacon with his orarion shews the priest the paten whereon lies the holy bread. In a low voice the priest continues: 'Likewise after supper He took the cup . . .' and as the deacon shews him the cup he says aloud: *Drink ye all of this: This is my blood of the new testament, which is shed for you and for many for the remission of sins.* And in the same manner the whole church cries aloud: *Amen.* [cf. *Mark xiv,* 24.]

The priest continues secretly: 'Remembering therefore this commandment of salvation, and all those things which came to pass for our sakes: the cross, the tomb, the resurrection on the third day, the ascension into heaven, the sitting on the right hand and the coming again a second time in glory: [Aloud] *Thine own, from Thine own, we offer unto Thee, in behalf of all, and for all.*' Laying aside the sacramental fan, the deacon lifts up the paten and the chalice —the sanctuary is no longer the upper chamber of the Last Supper, the altar is not the table but the place of offering— Golgotha, on which the Son of God offered Himself up in sacrifice for the whole world. The moment approaches both for the oblation and for each one to remember the sacrifice made by the Creator. We may incline before earthly authority; we may pay homage and respect and offer submission to men; but we make sacrifice to the Creator alone. Such sacrifice has been offered since the very day of the creation of the world and whatever the form of the sacrifice it was not the sacrifice itself which was required but the contrite spirit with which it was made. Therefore let each of those present bear in mind that at this moment the priest turns aside from the things of this world and puts away every extraneous idea, every earthly thought, like Abraham who, when he went up into the mountain to offer a burnt offering left in the valley below his wife and his servant and his ass, taking with him only the wood of the grievous confession of his transgressions to burn in the fire of his soul's repentance, with fire and the sword of the spirit slaying within himself every desire for earthly possessions and earthly good. But what are all our sacrifices before God when He says in the voice of the prophet: 'All our righteousnesses are as filthy rags'? (*Isa. lxiv*, 6.) Deeply conscious that there is nothing on earth worthy to be offered in sacrifice to God, all those present turn their thoughts to that same chalice which in the sanctuary the servant of the sanctuary raises on high, and each in the depths of his heart echoes: 'Thine own, from Thine own, we offer unto Thee, in behalf of all, and for all.' The choir sings: *We praise Thee, we bless Thee, we give thanks unto Thee, O Lord, and we pray unto Thee, our God.*

And the supreme moment of the whole Liturgy approaches: the transubstantiation. Within the sanctuary the threefold invocation of the Holy Spirit is made over the sacred gifts—the invocation of that same Holy Spirit by Which Christ was incarnate of the Virgin, by Which He died and rose again, and without Which the bread and the wine cannot be transformed into the Body and Blood of Christ.

Priest and deacon prostrate themselves three times before the altar, the priest each time praying in a low voice: 'O Lord, Who at the third hour didst send down Thy Holy Ghost upon Thine apostles: Take not the same from us, O God Who art good, but renew Him in us who make our supplications unto Thee.' Both accompany this invocation with the versicle: 'Create in me a clean heart, O God; and renew a right spirit within me.' (*Ps. li*, 10.) And after the second invocation: 'Cast me not away from thy presence; and take not thy holy spirit from me.' (*Ps. li*, 11.) And after the third invocation—'O Lord, Who at the third hour didst send down Thy Holy Spirit upon Thine apostles: Take not the same from us, O God Who art good, but renew Him in us who make our supplications unto Thee'—the deacon, bowing his head, points with his orarion to the holy bread and pronounces within himself 'Bless, Master, the holy bread.' The priest makes the sign of the cross three times over the holy bread. 'And make this bread the precious Body of Thy Christ.' The deacon exclaims *Amen*. And the Bread is now the very Body of Christ. Again, the deacon silently indicates the sacred chalice with his prayer-stole and says within himself: 'Bless, Master, the sacred chalice.' Blessing it, the priest prays 'And [make] that which is within this cup the precious Blood of Thy Christ.' The deacon responds *Amen*, and, pointing to both paten and chalice, says, 'Master, bless both.' And the priest blesses both, saying, 'Transmuting them by Thy Holy Spirit.' *Amen, amen, amen*, repeats the deacon. And on the altar now lie the Body and Blood—the transubstantiation is accomplished. A word has called forth the Eternal Word. The priest has slain not with a sword but with a word. Not the priest, in form and name like ourselves, but the Great and Eternal High Priest Himself has accomplished the sacrifice in His Person, as he accomplishes it eternally in the persons of His priests, in the same way as God said, 'Let there be light', and light shines eternally; and as God said, 'Let the earth bring forth grass', and the earth brings forth grass eternally. On the altar lies, not the likeness, not the appearance of the Body, but the very Body of the Lord—that Body which suffered on earth, was buffeted and spat upon, was crucified, buried, rose again, ascended with the Lord and sitteth on the right hand of the Father. The appearance of bread is preserved only that it may be food for men, and in that the Lord Himself said: 'I am the bread.' (*John vi*, 51.)

From the belfry the bell rings out to proclaim this great moment, so that every man wherever he may be—the traveller on the road, a labourer in the field, the man sitting at home or occupied elsewhere, the prisoner languishing in prison or the patient lying on a bed of sickness—may send up a prayer for himself too at this dread moment. All within the temple incline themselves to the ground before the Body and Blood of the Lord, calling upon Him in the words of the malefactor: 'Lord, remember me when thou comest into thy kingdom.' (*Luke xxiii*, 42.)

Bowing his head to the priest, the deacon says, 'Remember me, holy Master.' The priest answers: 'The Lord God remember thee in His kingdom always, now and for ever and unto ages of ages.' And the priest proceeds to the remembrance of all before the Lord, recalling the whole Church, both triumphant in heaven and militant here on earth, after the same manner and sequence as he prayed during the Offertory, beginning with the most holy Mother

of God, Whom the whole congregation glorifies with the
choir in a hymn of praise, as the Interceder for the entire
human race, the only one worthy by her great humility to
bear God within herself—that each of those present may
hear at this moment that the greatest virtue is humility,
and that God is incarnate in the heart of the humble one.
And after the Mother of God the prophets, apostles, fathers
of the Church are commemorated in the order as particles
were cut out for them during the Office of Oblation. After
them—all those who have departed this life, whose names
the deacon recites; then the living, beginning with those who
bear the heaviest burdens of responsibility, 'and that we in
their tranquillity may pass our days in rest and quietness, in
all godliness and soberness of life.' And the priest prays at
this time for all Christians here present, that the Merciful
One may pour down His mercy upon all, filling their
treasuries with every good thing, maintaining their marriage-
bonds in peace and concord, rearing the infants, guiding the
young, supporting the aged, comforting the faint-hearted,
gathering together the scattered and turning them from
their wandering and uniting them to His holy Catholick and
Apostolick Church. At this moment the priest humbly prays
for all Christians, down to the least of men, wherever he be
—journeying by land or by sea, in sickness or in suffering,
languishing in prison, in the mines and in bitter labours on
this earth. For all without exception the Church prays at
this time, and each of those present, over and above this
general supplication for all men, prays for those near to his
heart, murmuring their names in the presence of the Body
and Blood of the Lord. And the priest from the sanctuary
proclaims aloud: *And grant us with one mouth and one heart
to glorify and praise the majesty of Thy precious Name, of the*

Father, and of the Son, and of the Holy Spirit, now and for ever and unto ages of ages. The congregation responds with an affirmative *Amen.* The priest proclaims aloud: *And may the mercy of the great God, and our Saviour Jesus Christ, be with you all.—And with thy spirit,* sings the choir. And this ends the litany for all those who form the Church of Christ, performed in the presence of His very Body and Blood.

The deacon goes forth and stands in the customary place to pray for the Gifts which have been brought to God and transubstantiated, that they may not be turned to our judgment and condemnation. Lifting his prayer-stole with three fingers of his right hand, he exhorts all to pray: *Calling to remembrance all the saints, again and again let us pray unto the Lord!* And the choir responds: *Lord, have mercy.—For the precious gifts here set forth and hallowed, let us pray unto the Lord.* And the choir replies: *Lord, have mercy.—That our God, Who loveth mankind, Who hath received them unto His holy and heavenly and spiritual altar for a sweet savour of spiritual fragrance, may send down upon us in return His divine grace and the gift of the Holy Spirit, let us pray unto the Lord.—Lord, have mercy* responds the choir. *That we may be preserved from all tribulation, wrath and necessity, let us pray unto the Lord.—Lord, have mercy!—Protect us, save us, have mercy upon us and preserve us, O God, by Thy grace. —Lord, have mercy* chants the choir. *That our whole day may be perfect, holy, peaceful and without sin, we beseech Thee, O Lord.—Grant us, O Lord,* from the choir. *For an angel of peace, a faithful guide and guardian of our souls and bodies, we beseech Thee, O Lord.—Grant us, O Lord.—For pardon and remission of our sins and transgressions, we beseech Thee, O Lord.—Grant us, O Lord.—For things good and profitable to our souls, and peace to the world, let us beseech the Lord.—*

E

Grant us, O Lord!—That we may pass the remainder of our lives in peace and repentance, we beseech Thee, O Lord.—Grant us, O Lord.—For a Christian ending to our life, painless, peaceful and without shame, and a good defence before the dread Judgment Seat of Christ, we beseech Thee, O Lord.—Grant us, O Lord, sings the choir. And the deacon, no longer appealing to the saints for help but turning our attention to the Lord Himself, says: *Having besought the unity of the faith and the fellowship of the Holy Spirit, let us commend ourselves and one another and all our life unto Christ our God.—To Thee, O Lord*, chants the congregation in full and complete devotion.

And the priest, in place of the threefold doxology, exclaims: *And vouchsafe, O Lord, that boldly and without condemnation we may dare to lift our voices unto Thee, our God and heavenly Father, and say . . .* And all the faithful at this moment, not as servants filled with fear, but as children, as innocent babes, led by the litanies and the whole service and the gradual progress of its holy rites to the angelic, heavenly state when the heart is softened and moved and man can speak directly to God as to a loving father, say the Lord's Prayer: *Our Father which art in heaven, Hallowed be thy Name, Thy kingdom come, Thy will be done, in earth as it is in heaven. Give us this day our daily bread; And forgive us our trespasses, As we forgive them that trespass against us; And lead us not into temptation, But deliver us from evil.*

This prayer has embraced everything, and all our needs are included in it. In the petition 'Hallowed be thy Name' we ask the first thing, the thing we should desire above all else: where God's Name is kept holy, all is well, because people are living in love, for only in love can God's Name be hallowed. The words 'Thy kingdom come' invite the kingdom of righteousness on earth, for without the coming of God there can be no righteousness, for God is righteousness. Faith and reason lead man to pray 'Thy will be done'—whose will can be more excellent than God's? Who better than the Creator Himself knows what His creature needs? To whom entrust oneself if not to Him, Who is all beneficent goodness and perfection? 'Give us this day our daily bread'—thus we pray for all that is needful in our daily existence. Our bread is the wisdom of God, is Christ Himself, Who said: 'I am the living bread ... if any man eat of this bread, he shall live for ever.' (*John vi*, 51.) By the words 'Forgive us our trespasses' we ask for deliverance from the burden of our sins which weigh us down; we ask forgiveness for our transgressions against our brethren, and therefore against the Creator Himself, Who through them at every moment holds out His Hand to us, begging for mercy and kindness. 'Lead us not into temptation'—here we ask to be spared from all that troubles our soul and deprives us of spiritual peace. In the words 'But deliver us from evil' we pray for heavenly joy, for immediately the evil one leaves us joy floods the soul, and though on earth we are as it were in heaven.

Thus all is provided for and embraced in this prayer, which the Wisdom of God Himself taught us to pray. And to Whom do we pray it? To the Father of Wisdom, Who begat His Wisdom before all worlds. And just as all present should repeat this prayer to themselves, not with lips but with the pure innocent heart of a child, so should the singing of it be childlike. The choir should chant, not in vigorous, loud tones, but gently, letting the prayer caress the soul, bringing with it the spring-like breath of heaven and the salutation of the angels, for in this prayer we no longer address our Creator as God but say to Him 'Our Father'.

E*

From the depths of the sanctuary the priest sends forth the greeting of the Saviour: *Peace be with you all.—And with thy spirit,* answers the choir. Reminding us that at this moment we should be making our confession secretly in our hearts, the deacon exclaims: *Bow your heads unto the Lord.* And bowing our heads with one accord we utter within ourselves such a prayer as this: 'To Thee, O Lord my God, do I bow my head, and in sincere confession cry: I have sinned, O Lord, and am not worthy to ask Thy forgiveness, but Thou dost love mankind. Do Thou, therefore, pardon me, as Thou didst pardon the prodigal son. Justify me as Thou didst justify the publican, and bestow on me like the malefactor Thy kingdom of heaven.' And while the congregation stands thus with bowed heads and contrite hearts the priest within the sanctuary prays silently for all: 'We give thanks unto Thee, O King invisible, Who by Thy measureless power hast fashioned all things, and in the multitude of Thy mercies hast from non-existence brought all things into existence. Look down, O Lord, from heaven upon those who bow their heads to Thee, for they have bowed not to flesh and blood but to Thee, O dread God. Bestow on us, therefore, O Lord, these Thy Gifts, giving to each according to his need. Sail with them that sail upon the seas; journey with them that travel on dry land; and heal the sick, O Thou Who art the Physician of our souls and bodies.' Whereupon he pronounces aloud the great doxology of the Trinity, addressed to the heavenly mercy of God: *Through the bountiful grace and love toward mankind of Thine only-begotten Son, with Whom, together with Thy most holy, good and life-giving Spirit, Thou art blessed now and for ever and unto ages of ages.* The choir chants *Amen* and the priest, preparing to communicate himself and afterwards the people in the Body and Blood of Christ, prays the secret prayer: 'Hear us, O Lord Jesus Christ our God, from Thy holy habitation and from the glorious throne of Thy kingdom. Come forth to hallow us, Thou that sittest on high with the Father and art here invisibly present with us; and vouchsafe by Thy mighty Hand to impart unto us, Thy priests, Thy most holy Body and most precious Blood, and by us unto all Thy people.'

While the priest is saying this prayer the deacon prepares himself for Communion: he stands before the Royal Gates, girds his stole about him crosswise, in the likeness of the angels folding their wings crosswise to cover their faces before the unapproachable light of the Godhead. Bowing thrice, like the priest, he pronounces thrice within his heart: 'O God, cleanse me a sinner and have mercy upon me.' When the priest stretches forth his hand to the holy paten the deacon cries: *Let us give heed*, exhorting all present to fix their thoughts on that which is taking place. The sanctuary is now concealed from the gaze of the people, the curtain is drawn, for the Communion of the clergy. Only the voice of the priest within the sanctuary is heard during the elevation, as he proclaims: *Holy things unto the holy*! Trembling at these words which proclaim that all must be holy who would receive the holy things, the congregation of the faithful responds: *One only is holy, One only is the Lord, Jesus Christ, to the glory of God the Father.* [cf. *Rev. xv*, 4; *Eph. iv*, 5]. There follows a hymn in praise of the saint whose day it is, to tell us that it is possible for a man to become holy, just as the saint we sing became holy—not with his own holiness but with the holiness of Christ Himself. Dwelling in Christ hallows a man. While he abides in Christ he is holy, in the same way as iron in the furnace takes on the quality of fire but reverts to its former condition of sombre metal as soon as it is withdrawn.

The priest now breaks the Holy Bread, at first according to the marks traced during the Office of Oblation, into four pieces, saying reverently: 'The Lamb of God is broken and distributed, Which being broken is not divided, being ever eaten is never consumed, but sanctifieth them that partake thereof.' And he reserves one of these pieces for his own Communion and that of the deacon, separately from the Blood, and then divides the other parts according to the number of communicants; yet in this dividing the very Body of Christ is undivided, of Whom not a bone was broken, and in the minutest of particles is preserved the same whole Christ [cf. *John xix*, 36], just as in each member of our body the spirit of the whole man is present—not a part but whole and inseparable; just as a mirror, though broken into a thousand fragments, reflects the same objects, even with its smallest splinter; just as the sounds we hear remain the same complete sounds though heard by a thousand ears. But all the portions which were taken out at the Oblation in commemoration of the saints, in remembrance of the dead and in intercession for the living are not put into the chalice but are left for the time being on the paten; the Church uses only the portions constituting the Body and Blood of the Lord for the Communion. In the first days of Christianity the sacred Elements were partaken of separately. Now only the clergy communicate thus, each one receiving into his hands the Body of the Lord and afterwards drinking from the chalice. But when the ignorant and newly converted Christians, who were such only in name, began to carry the holy Gifts to their homes and put them to superstitious and sorcerous uses, or behave irreverently with them while in church, jostling each other, making a noise and even spilling the sacred Elements, and the fathers of many of the churches found it necessary to give Communion in the form of bread only—a wafer, as did the Roman Church in the west— St John Chrysostom decreed (lest this should happen in the Eastern Church) that the Body and Blood should be given to the people, not separately, but in a united form; and not into their hands but with the holy spoon, serving as it were as the image of the tongs with which the flaming seraphim touched the lips of the prophet Isaiah [cf. *Isa. vi*, 6, 7], in order to remind all of the nature of this touching of their mouths, in order that each may see that in this sacred spoon the priest holds the live coal which with mystic tongs the seraphim took from off the very altar of God, to lay upon the lips of the prophet and thereby purge his sins. Lest any should think that this putting together and uniting of the Body and Blood be arbitrarily done by the clergy St John Chrysostom ordained that warm water should be poured into the vessel at the same time as the Elements, signifying the warmth of the grace of the Holy Spirit being poured in to unite the Elements. Wherefore the deacon pronounces the words: 'The fervour of faith, full of the Holy Spirit.' And the blessing of the same Holy Spirit is called upon the warm water, so that nothing be done without the blessing of the Lord Himself and that the warm water also serve as a symbol of the warmth of blood, making all who taste of it realise that the blood they drink comes not from a dead body—warm blood does not flow from a dead body—but from the living, life-giving Body of the Lord. The warmth is a sign that the divine soul did not leave the dead body of the Lord, which was full of the action of the Spirit and not parted from the Godhead.

Having communicated first himself and then the deacon, the minister of Christ stands forth a new man, purified by communion with the holy things of all his transgressions, in truth a saint at this moment, worthy to communicate others.

The Royal Gates are opened, the deacon lifts up his voice and cries solemnly: *In the fear of God and with faith draw near*. And like a transfigured seraph holding the sacred chalice in his hands the priest appears between the Royal Gates.

Athirst for God, burning with love for Him, with hands crossed upon the breast, one after the other the communicants approach and with bent head repeat each to himself the confession of faith in the Crucified:

'I believe, O Lord, and confess that Thou art in truth the Christ, Son of the living God, come into the world to save sinners, of whom I am chief. And I believe that this is Thy most pure Body, and this Thy most precious Blood. Wherefore I pray Thee, have mercy upon me, and forgive me my trespasses, voluntary and involuntary, whether of word or of deed, witting or unwitting, and vouchsafe that I may partake without condemnation of Thy most pure Mysteries, for the remission of sins and unto life everlasting.' Pausing for a moment to grasp the significance of what he is about to do, he then continues from the depths of his heart:

'Of Thy mystical Supper, O Son of God, accept me this day as a partaker: for I will not speak of the Mystery to Thine enemies, nor will I give Thee a kiss like Judas, but like the thief I will acknowledge Thee: Remember me, O Lord, in Thy kingdom.' And after a moment's reverent silence he goes on: 'And let not this participation in Thy

Holy Mysteries be to my judgment nor to my condemnation, but unto the healing of soul and body.'

And having made this confession, each one approaches, not as to a priest but as to a flaming seraph—ready with open lips to receive from the sacred spoon the live coal of the Holy Body and Blood of the Lord, which is to burn away like dead brushwood all the black dross of his transgressions, driving eternal night from his soul and transforming him into a shining seraph. And when, raising the sacred spoon to his mouth and pronouncing his name, the priest says: *The servant of God* [naming the communicant], *partaketh of the precious and holy Body and Blood of our Lord and God and Saviour Jesus Christ, for the remission of his sins and unto life everlasting*, he receives the Body and Blood of the Lord, and in them he meets God, coming face to Face with Him. In this moment time does not exist. In nothing does it differ from eternity itself, since He Who is the source of eternity abides therein. Having received this great moment in the Body and Blood, the communicant stands in holy awe. With the sacred *aer* his mouth is wiped, accompanied by the words of the seraph to the prophet Isaiah: 'Lo, this hath touched thy lips; and thine iniquity is taken away, and thy sin purged.' (*Isa. vi*, 7.) Now made holy himself, he turns away from the sacred chalice, bowing in salutation to the holy things and bowing to the people in the congregation as closer far to his heart now that he is bound to them by ties of holy, heavenly affinity, and stands in his place, filled with the thought that he has taken Christ Himself into him and Christ Himself is in him, that Christ in His flesh has entered into him, into the very womb of his heart, as into a grave, so that, penetrating into the secret depths of his heart, He may rise again in his spirit, accomplishing within him both His Burial and His Resurrection. The whole church shines radiant with the light of this spiritual resurrection, and the choir chants this joyous hymn:

We have beheld the Resurrection of Christ, wherefore let us bow down before the Lord Jesus, for that He is holy, He only is without sin. Thy Cross, O Christ, we worship, and Thy holy Resurrection we laud and glorify; for Thou art our God, and we know none other beside Thee; we call upon Thy Name. O come, all ye faithful, let us bow down and worship Christ's holy Resurrection; for behold by the Cross is joy come into all the world. Ever blessing the Lord, let us sing His Resurrection; for in that He endured the Cross death by death hath He destroyed.

And again, with the choir of angels who now join their song to ours:

Shine, shine, O new Jerusalem, for the glory of the Lord is risen upon thee. Rejoice now and be glad, O Zion. And do thou, O pure Mother of God, appear in thy splendour, for He Whom thou didst bear is risen. O Christ, O great and most sacred Passover! O Wisdom and Power of God! Grant us more truly to partake of Thee, in that day of Thy kingdom which shall have no night.

As a sequel to the anthems of resurrection sung by the rejoicing church the priest within the closed sanctuary, having placed the sacred chalice on the holy table, covering it and the paten with the veils again, says the prayer of thanksgiving to the Lord and Benefactor of our souls that He has deemed us worthy of His heavenly and immortal Mysteries. The priest concludes with the petition that God will make straight our path, confirm us in all holy awe of Him, watch over our life and make safe our ways.

The Royal Gates open for the last time, signifying the

opening of the Kingdom of Heaven itself, which Christ obtained for all men by the giving of Himself as spiritual food for the whole world. In the sacred chalice which the deacon brought out with the words 'In the fear of God and with faith draw near', and which is now borne away, we see symbolised the coming of the Lord to the people in order to lead all with Him to His Father's house. In triumphant tones the choir thunders forth *Blessed is He that cometh in the name of the Lord. God is the Lord and hath appeared unto us.* Turning to the people, the priest blesses them with the words *O God save Thy people, and bless Thine inheritance*, for he conceives that all, at this moment, in their purity have become the inheritance of God. Then he lifts his thoughts to the Ascension with which the Lord closed His sojourn on earth. Standing with the deacon before the holy altar and doing reverence, he censes it for the last time, repeating to himself: 'Be Thou exalted, O God, above the heavens; let thy glory be above all the earth.' (*Ps. lvii,* 5.) Meanwhile the choir, with exultant anthems, thrilling with spiritual gladness, inspires the congregation of the faithful, their souls radiant, to repeat these words of rejoicing: 'We have beheld the true Light, we have received the heavenly Spirit, we have found the true Faith. Let us bow down and worship the Trinity Undivided, for the Same hath saved us.'

The deacon appears between the Royal Gates holding the sacred paten above his head. He utters no word, but in silence glances towards the congregation, and by his withdrawal signifies the Lord's withdrawal and Ascension. Immediately after the deacon the priest appears between the Royal Gates with the sacred chalice, and with the words *Always, now and for ever and unto ages of ages* proclaims the risen Lord's presence with us to the end of time. Both chalice and paten are now borne back to the offertory table where the Office of Oblation was performed and which now represents, not the grotto of the Nativity of Christ, but glory on high whither the Son returned to the bosom of the Father.

The whole church, led by the choir, now joins in a hymn of solemn thanksgiving: *Let our mouths be filled with Thy praise, O Lord, that we may sing of Thy glory, for that Thou hast vouchsafed to make us partakers of Thy holy, divine, immortal and life-giving Mysteries. Preserve us in Thy holiness that all the day long we may learn Thy righteousness.* At the end the choir sings a threefold *Alleluia*, telling of the unceasing care and presence of God everywhere. The deacon advances to the tribune in order for the last time to exhort the people to a prayer of thanksgiving. Raising his orarion between three fingers, he cries: *Be upright. Having partaken of the divine, holy, spotless, immortal, heavenly, life-giving and terrible Mysteries of Christ, we give worthy thanks unto the Lord.* And with thankful hearts all respond softly, *Lord, have mercy.—Protect us, save us, have mercy upon us and preserve us, O God, by Thy grace* prays the deacon for the last time. *Lord, have mercy* echo the faithful. *Beseeching that our whole day may be perfect, holy, peaceful and without sin, let us commend ourselves and one another and all our life to Christ our God.* And with the humility of a submissive child trusting in God all exclaim: *To Thee, O Lord!* Meanwhile the priest, having folded the corporal, or communion cloth, and made the sign of the cross over it with the book of the Gospels, pronounces the doxology of the Trinity which has shone like a beacon through the whole progress of the Divine Service, and now flashes more brightly still in our enlightened souls. This time the form of the ascription is: *For Thou art our sanctification, and unto Thee we ascribe glory, unto Father, Son and Holy Spirit, now and for ever and unto ages of ages.*

The priest now goes to the side altar on which the chalice and paten have been placed. All the particles which have remained on the paten and were taken out at the Office of Oblation in memory of the saints, for the repose of the dead and the spiritual health of the living are now put into the sacred chalice and by this action Christ's whole Church communicates in His Body and Blood—both the Church still militant here on earth and the Church now triumphant in heaven. The Mother of God, the prophets, apostles, fathers of the Church, saints, anchorites, martyrs and all sinful men, both the living and the departed, for whom particles were taken out, communicate at this moment in Christ's Body and Blood. And the priest, standing at this moment before God, as the representative of His Church, drains this universal communion from the chalice and taking into himself this communion prays for all, that they may be washed of their sins, for Christ made His sacrifice for the redemption of all—alike for those who lived before and those born after His coming. And however sinful his prayer may be, the priest offers it up for all, even for the most saintly, for, as St John Chrysostom said, redemption is for the whole universe.

The Church commands that common prayer be made for all. The great importance and stern necessity of such prayer were recognised, not by the wise men of the world, not by the 'disputers' of the age [cf. 1 *Cor. i*, 20], but by those supreme beings whose high spiritual perfection and angelic lives led them to knowledge of the deepest spiritual mysteries and showed them plainly that there is no separation among those living in God—that the passing corruptibility of our bodies does not interrupt our association, and that love which bound us on earth expands and grows stronger in heaven, its natural home, and that the brother who has gone from us becomes still closer to us by the force of love. And all that flows from Christ is as eternal as its source is Himself eternal. By their higher discernment these sovereign beings became aware that the Church triumphant in heaven must needs pray, and does pray for her pilgrim brethren on earth; that God has bestowed on the Church the greatest delectation—the delight of prayer, for God performs no action and gives no good thing without making His creature a participator in the work and the benefaction, that the created may enjoy the bliss of doing good. An angel does His bidding and is blissful in doing it. The saint in heaven prays for his brethren on earth and is fraught with bliss in praying. And all share with God in His delights and His bliss. Multitudes of the most perfect creatures proceed from the hands of God, that they may have a part in ever higher blessedness, and there is no end to them, as there is no end to the blessedness of God.

Having drained the chalice of the Communion of all with God, the priest brings out to the people the altar bread from which the particles were cut and separated,[1] and thus is preserved the ancient rite of the early Christian Agape. Although the table is no longer laid for the feast, because ignorant Christians, by their noisy rejoicing, their quarrelling, long ago dishonoured the holiness of this moving heavenly banquet in the very house of God, at which all the guests were holy and of one soul, and, like innocent

[1] For communion and commemoration. [Tr.]

children, their conversation was as the conversation in heaven with God Himself; although the Church herself was compelled to abolish the custom, and the very memory of it has disappeared in many places, the Eastern Church however could not bring herself to do away with the rite entirely, and in the distribution of the holy bread she fulfils the same holy feast of love. Wherefore each one who receives a *prosphora* accepts it as bread from that feast at which the Creator of the world Himself spoke to His people —and so he should eat it reverently, thinking of himself as surrounded by all men as by his dearest brethren. And, as was the custom in the primitive Church, he eats it before any other food, or carries it home to his family, or gives it to the sick, the poor, or such as were for some reason unable to come to church.

Having distributed the holy bread, the priest proceeds to the dismissal, and blesses the people with the words: *May Christ our true God, by the prayers of His most pure Mother, by the prayers of our father and archbishop John Chrysostom* (if the Liturgy of St John Chrysostom has been used), *by the prayers of St N.* (and here he names the saint whose day it is) *and of all the saints, have mercy upon us and save us, for He is good and He loveth mankind.* The faithful make the sign of the cross over themselves and bow, and disperse to the loud singing by the choir of 'Unto length of days . . .' for the Emperor.

The priest within the sanctuary unvests, saying as he does so: 'Lord, now lettest thou my servant depart in peace,' and accompanies his unrobing by hymns of praise to the holy father and prelate whose liturgy has been celebrated, and to the most-holy Virgin in whom was incarnate Him in Whose honour the Liturgy has been said. The deacon, meanwhile, consumes all that remains in the chalice, and afterwards pouring wine and water into it washes the inside of the chalice and drinks the ablutions, carefully dries the inside with the sponge that nothing should be left; places the holy vessels together, covers and binds them together, and says, like the priest, the *Nunc Dimittis*, and repeats the same hymns and prayers. And both leave the church, radiant in face and joyful in spirit, and with thanksgiving to the Lord on their lips.

EPILOGUE

THE influence of the Divine Liturgy on the soul is profound. Celebrated visibly and openly, in the sight of all the world, it is yet hidden. If the worshipper will only follow each act reverently and attentively, obedient to the bidding of the deacon, his soul will be attuned to lofty things, he will find it possible to fulfil the commandments of Christ, the yoke of Christ will be easy and His burden light. On leaving the church where he has been present at the divine feast of love he looks on all men as brethren. Whether he returns to his daily task in business or in the family, whatever or wherever it be, his spirit will involuntarily retain the lofty imprint of loving fellowship with all men as brought from heaven by the God-Man. He will be more lenient and kind to his subordinates. If he be under the authority of another he will obey the more readily and happily, as he would obey the Saviour Himself. If he sees one in need his heart will be more disposed to help than at any other time: he will feel greater delight in giving and give the more lovingly. If he himself be needy he will thankfully accept the least bounty: his heart will be touched and overflow with gratitude, and never will he pray more fervently for his benefactor than now. And all who have diligently followed the Divine Liturgy emerge gentler, kindlier in their dealings with others, friendlier, quieter in behaviour.

And therefore everyone who desires to advance and become better should be present as frequently as possible at the Divine Liturgy, carefully following every word. The Liturgy imperceptibly forms and develops a man. If society still holds together, if people do not breathe complete, irreconcilable hatred for one another, the reason lies hidden in the Divine Liturgy, which reminds man of holy, heavenly love towards his brother. Wherefore, if any would be confirmed in love, he must as often as possible frequent in awe, faith and love the sacred Love-feast; and if he feels unworthy to receive within himself the very God Who is all love, let him at least witness when others communicate, that he may unconsciously, insensibly advance a step each week towards perfection.

Great and incalculable may be the influence of the Divine Liturgy if we will only be present and listen, resolved to put what we hear into practice in our lives.

Instructing all alike, acting alike on each link of the chain, from the sovereign to the lowest beggar, the Liturgy speaks the same message to all, though perhaps not in one and the same tongue, teaches to all that love which is the bond of society, the hidden spring of all which moves in harmony, the love that is all food, all life.

But if the Divine Liturgy acts so strongly on those present at its celebration how much more powerfully does it affect the priest who celebrates. If he has celebrated reverently, in awe, faith and love, he is now all purified, like the vessels of the Temple, not now to be put to any unclean use . . . In the fulfilment of his many and various pastoral duties, at home with his family or among his parishioners, who are also his family, the Saviour Himself will be represented in him, and Christ will be in all he does, and in his every word Christ will speak. Whether he set himself to make peace among those at enmity, urge the strong to be merciful to the weak, or soften the hard-hearted, comfort the sorrowful, encourage the suffering to be patient—his words will acquire the healing power of oil, and will everywhere be words of peace and love.